The publication of this book is sponsored by Gallier House, New Orleans, Louisiana, as part of a continuing program of study and interpretation of American life in the nineteenth century.

Gallier House is an educational complex comprised of an historic restoration of the French Quarter residence and garden of New Orleans architect, James Gallier, Jr., an adjacent museum building in which changing exhibits explore urban life in the nineteenth century, and an administrative building with educational and curatorial facilities.

James Gallier, Jr., built his home in 1857. His family included his wife and four young daughters. Four servants were also part of the Gallier household. Recreating the style of this lively group through historically accurate furnishings, artifacts, architectural details and landscaping is the intent of the Gallier House restoration project.

The Gallier House complex was first opened to the public in 1971. It has been designated a National Historic Landmark by the Department of Interior, and has been accredited by the American Association of Museums. Gallier House is funded by the Ella West Freeman Foundation of New Orleans.

The Athenaeum of Philadelphia was founded in 1814 "for the purpose of collecting historical and other monuments, connected with the history and antiquities of America, and the useful arts, and generally to disseminate useful knowledge." In 1968, The Athenaeum joined with The Victorian Society, whose offices are in The Athenaeum's building, to offer a national program of research and publication based on its heretofore largely unknown rare collections developed over the past 160 years.

The Athenaeum is housed in the first major American building in the Italianate Revival Style, designed for the Library by John Notman, and erected near Independence Hall in 1845-1847. This handsome structure has recently been restored and expanded to provide fireproof facilities for a rapidly growing collection of architectural drawings, photographs, prints, manuscripts, and rare books devoted to nineteenth century social and cultural history.

In recent years, The Athenaeum has attracted substantial new collections from all parts of the country. As a Public Charity, donations to The Athenaeum of appropriate research materials are tax deductible at appraised value. The collections are made available without charge to all qualified persons studying the last century.

The original copy of *Exterior Decoration* used for this new edition is from the Dornsife collection of The Victorian Society in America at The Athenaeum of Philadelphia.

The Victorian Society was founded in 1966 to promote an awareness and appreciation of Victorian culture, architecture, decorative arts, design, and craftsmanship, and to encourage their protection and preservation.

The Society is supported by its membership and publishes *Nineteenth Century*, an illustrated magazine with articles concerning Victorian life and culture, and The VSA *Bulletin*, a bi-monthly newsletter containing current news and reports of coming events, activities, and special items of interest.

An Annual Tour and Meeting is held in a city where Victoriana is dominant. The Victorian Society also sponsors an Annual Workshop, on the social and cultural aspects of life in nineteenth century America, and an annual summer study tour in England.

In addition to the national program, the Society has chartered over a dozen local chapters with active programs of their own. The rapid growth of the VSA reflects an increasing interest in our Victorian heritage.

EXTERIOR DECORATION.

A TREATISE ON THE ARTISTIC USE OF COLORS IN THE ORNAMENTATION OF BUILDINGS,

AND

A SERIES OF DESIGNS,

Illustrating the Effects of Different Combinations of Colors in Connection with Various Styles of Architecture.

With a new introduction by Samuel J. Dornsife, A.S.I.D.

The Athenaeum Library of Nineteenth Century America
The Athenaeum of Philadelphia
1976

Library of Congress Catalog Card No.: 75-22528

ISBN: 0-916530-00-0
ISBN: 0-89257-000-8

Exterior decoration, Victorian paint for Victorian houses. Philadelphia, The Athenaeum of Philadelphia, 1976.
90 p. illus., color chips, bibliography.
  1. Athenaeum Library of Nineteenth Century America.
  2. F. W. Devoe & Co.
  3. Samuel Jonathan Dornsife, 1916—.
  4. Trade Catalogs—Paint.
  5. Paint—Industry and Trade.

Contents

Note: At the end of the book will be found two pages upon which are mounted fifty paint samples keyed to the plates by number. They are preceeded by a statistical analysis and index as well as twenty alternate color schemes.

New Foreword

Exterior Decoration is the first publication in a new series entitled THE ATHENAEUM LIBRARY OF NINETEENTH CENTURY AMERICA. It is the joint effort of three educational institutions sharing a common devotion to that age called Victorian. The Gallier House is a brilliantly restored museum complex in New Orleans, and The Victorian Society in America is a national organization with broad member programs that foster an appreciation of Victorian life and culture. The Athenaeum of Philadelphia is one of America's oldest independent literary societies, and the only research library devoted exclusively to the study of nineteenth century social and cultural history.

The purpose of this book and those following in the series is to make available rare primary documents on nineteenth century architecture and decoration for which curators, collectors, architects and preservationists have a practical need. Topics of books in production or planned for the future include: drapery design, architectural ironwork, lighting fixtures, Gothic Revival furniture, plumbing, kitchens and architectural pattern books.

Color documentation is one of the most difficult problems facing the owner of a period house who wants to paint it authentically. The choice of Victorian coloration as the first topic in the series then comes as no surprise. As Mr. Dornsife remarks in the following introduction, it is nearly impossible for two people to discuss color without an actual sample as a point of reference. Ideally a restoration should be based on a careful, detailed microanalysis of original painted surfaces, but such scientific archaeology is expensive, and there are few persons qualified to conduct the studies.

The Athenaeum has been gathering works on Victorian paint in an effort to meet the growing demand for accurate color documentation where microanalysis is not possible. We have found most useful the color cards issued by the manufacturers of ready-mixed paint, especially counter-top

display books that graphically demonstrate the application of their products on houses of the period. (Occasionally customers were even shown how to "modernize" with paint. See Plates XIII and XIV.) These books are the ideal primary document. The houses themselves are shown by handsome lithographs, usually keyed by number to chips of actual paint, and the color relationship for body and trim are clearly delineated.

It is one thing to have gathered such sources at The Athenaeum, but quite another to help the individual for whom a trip to Philadelphia is clearly impracticable. The usual tools of microfilm and Xerox, by which a research library provides copies from fragile, non-circulating materials, are useless. Even photography and modern color printing have their limitations when dealing with heavily pigmented dark shades of subtle gradation. (This is especially true for late nineteenth century colors that were purposely "muddy.") The only way to overcome these technical problems was to take a cue from paint manufacturers, past as well as present, and produce an actual display book, complete with color plates and paint chips carefully matched to the nineteenth century originals. Fortunately we were able to secure the assistance of the firm that had produced *Exterior Decoration* in 1885. The Devoe Paint Company referred us to the Matherson-Selig Company of Chicago whose technical staff studied the colors by spectroscope and blended modern paint to reproduce them exactly. In an act of enlightened corporate generosity, the Devoe Paint Company contributed enough sets of the resulting chips for our edition; without this help the book you now hold would not have been possible.

In our estimation, *Exterior Decoration* is the most important and informative of the several paint books that have survived and are listed in the bibliography. Other books, the John Lucas & Co. *Portfolio of Modern House Painting Designs* (1887), for example, are larger, and there are numerous smaller books and a legion of single sheet paint cards. Paint cards did not, unfortunately, become widely available until the 1870s. It is therefore important that Mr. Dornsife's introduction be studied carefully. Between the universal white-trimed-with-green of the first half of the century (Plate XIII), and the darker shades of the post-Centennial period, there is an intervening quarter century of lighter drab, grey and fawn coloration for which only written documentation exists, save for rare colored plate pattern books like John Riddell's *Architectural Designs for Model Country Residences* (1864). It would be as inconsistent to use the dark palette of *Exterior Decoration* on a structure of c.1850 as it would be to paint it white with green trim.

The earliest large paint card we have found was issued by Harrison Brothers in 1871. Inasmuch as this card predates *Exterior Decoration* by over a decade, it has been reproduced here to broaden our coverage of Victorian coloration. (Reprinting the Harrison Brothers card was made possible by combining plates XVII and XVIII of *Exterior Decoration*.) For ease of reference, the colors have been identified by number with the Munsell Color System by Mr. Frank Welsh of Ardmore, Pennsylvania.

In addition to Mr. Dornsife's introduction, bibliography and the Harrison Brothers color card, this book includes at the end twenty alternative paint schemes based on the Lucas *Portfolio* and keyed by number to the color chips at the end of the book. Two of the schemes are adaptations to utilize some of the original colors not displayed on Plates I-XX or used in the Lucas line. At the end will be found a summary of use for each of the fifty colors in the original *Exterior Decoration,* from which it becomes immediately apparent that certain colors were used quite often (dark brown, for example). Two colors are not used by either Devoe or Lucas and deserve special mention. Color number 584 is a bright blue that would have been used *sparingly as an accent only,* not as a body or major trim color. It might be used for commercial store fronts where it would be thought useful to drawn attention. Color number 586 is a bright red that was used in the 1880s and 1890s to paint the *putty* on a dark sash. The resulting fine red outline around the glass was not obvious from any distance, yet enlivened the overall effect of the completed color scheme. *It would never have been used as a body or overall trim color.* In modest quantities it might have been used to "pick out" small details.

There is one final caution concerning the color plates which are remarkably close to the originals. In comparing the lithographs with the color chips, a rather disquieting casualness was discovered in the originals. A plate may illustrate, say, a dark body color and a light trim, while the facing page called for the opposite placement. "We regard our Plates only as suggestions, upon which the painter can enlarge at pleasure to such an extent as the colors at his command will allow. . . ." Nor is the color match between plates and chips sufficiently reliable in the original; the nineteenth century printer had less control over his inks than modern pressmen. Consequently, readers are cautioned to work from the paint chips rather than the plates when selecting colors. The plates serve best today as in 1885: "as a means of illustrating the effects that can be produced by a judicious and artistic use of colors. . . ."

No production so complex as *Exterior Decoration* could have been possible without the interest and effort of many people who deserve thanks: Nadine Russell, Curator, Gallier House, and Frank A. M. Williams, Executive Director, The Ella West Freeman Foundation, New Orleans, Louisiana; John C. Freeman, Director, the American Life Foundation, Watkins Glen, New York; J. P. Cotter, Executive Vice-President, Valley Offset, Inc., Deposit, New York; L. L. Beard, Devoe Paint Division, Celanese Coatings & Specialties Company, Louisville, Kentucky; Earl Ogier, Executive Vice-President, Matherson-Selig Company, Chicago, Illinois; Frank Welsh, Ardmore, Pennsylvania; Joseph Van Why, Director, Stowe-Day Foundation, Hartford, Connecticut; William J. Murtagh, President, and Joan Thill, Executive Director, The Victorian Society in America; George Vaux, President, and the Directors and staff, The Athenaeum of Philadelphia.

Finally, a special thanks to Samuel J. Dornsife, Williamsport, Pennsylvania, for providing the introduction that follows and for nearly forty years of lonely collecting and research before the rest of us discovered Victorian studies.

ROGER W. MOSS, JR.
The Athenaeum of Philadelphia

INTRODUCTION

by SAMUEL J. DORNSIFE

Among the earliest and most frequently quoted sources for the mid-nineteenth century use of color are the writings of Andrew Jackson Downing, who originally indicated his aversion to white exterior paint trimmed with bright green blinds in *Cottage Residences* (New York, 1842). He suggested instead the use of grey and drab or fawn colors, and gave six specimen tints on a hand water-colored plate. These opinions were elaborated upon in *Architecture of Country Houses* (New York, 1850), when Downing again expressed opposition to white exterior paint trimmed with bright green and argued for the use of neutral shades. He also recommended that a large house in a prominent and exposed position should be painted darker colors than a smaller house in a more concealed position.

Others picked up Downing's ideas. Henry W. Cleaveland, William and Samuel D. Backus, in their *Village and Farm Cottages* (New York, 1856), wrote:

In regard to colors, there is a boundless diversity of taste, and this perhaps is well, for it insures variety. No rule can be given. Houses differing essentially in character and situation, ought not to be painted alike. White seems to be the general favorite. Yet this, for a near and constant object of sight, is not pleasing or kindly to the eye. Neither do we like, especially for rural dwellings, the darker shades. The needed variety may be found among the softer, lighter, and more cheerful tints; tints which neither pain the eye by their glare, nor repel it by their gloom.

Another Downing disciple was Gervase Wheeler, who in his *Homes for the People* (New York, 1855), recommended the use of neutral colors and the painting of inferior grades of brick. "Cornices, window dressings, verandah mouldings, &c., might be made more prominent by coloring them a shade darker than the main building, though this step must be taken with great caution, so as to not divide the house by stripes, or produce too marked a line of contrast." For one of his designs he recommended the use of a body color approaching what would result from mixing a teaspoon full of strong coffee in a cup of cream, while the tin roofs of the same house be painted a cool grey, something between the color of the house and a lead color.

After giving recipes for mixing these colors, Wheeler states that the shade "will be changed by the addition of sand, which in all cases is recommended, in a proportion of about one quart to every one hundred pounds of mixed color. The finest and whitest sand that the neighborhood affords should be used, and as its hue differs so will the tint of the paint be changed.

The adding of sand to exterior paint was quite common in the mid-nineteenth century. In 1847, the architect John Notman had his painters color the massive wooden cornice of The Athenaeum of Philadelphia grey, into which was mixed ample quantities of fine white sand. Downing suggests blending fifty pounds of "finely sifted sharp clean sand" with the same weight of white lead, ten quarts of linseed oil, one half pound of Dryers', two pounds of raw umber, and half a pint of turpentine. This mixture is then applied "with a *large* brush. I use a *wire* brush, which does not cut through with the sand." Gervase Wheeler writes that "sanding paint, or mixing sand therewith, besides assisting in its preservation, takes away from the oily glare and glisten of ordinary pigments, and by lessening the refracting power, gives to the surface of the building a softer and more pleasant tone of coloring. But I do not recommend the process in all cases, believing in no universal rule that admits not of exception; frequently where the detail is minute, the roughened appearance imparted by the use of sand gives a clumsy aspect to the part, and in all cases where sharpness of outline is sought to be obtained by any particular decoration of the construction, the use of sand would be particularly inadmissable. . . . Sometimes one sees iron sanded in imitation of stone;—many iron railings in New York are so finished,—he would be a cunning mason who could cut such splinters of Connecticut brown-stone!" Contrary to this criticism, many iron architectural castings and shop fronts were very effectively and practically sanded.

Calvert Vaux, in his *Villas and Cottages* (New York, 1857), followed the new coloration:

The question of color is a most interesting one in any design for a country house, and seems at present but little understood in America, by far the greater number of houses being simply painted white, with bright green blinds. By this means each residence is distinctly protruded from the surrounding scenery, and instead of grouping and harmonizing with it, asserts a right to carry on a separate business on its own account; and this lack of sympathy between the building and its surroundings is very disagreeable to an artistic eye. Even a harsh, vulgar outline may often pass without particular notice in a view of rural scenery, if the mass is quiet and harmonious in color; while a very tolerable composition may injure materially the views near it if it is painted white, the human eye being so constituted that it will be constantly held in bondage by this striking blot of crude light, and compelled to give it unwilling attention.

Thus, concludes Vaux, "the colors of rural buildings should be carefully varied. They should be often cheerful and light, sometimes neutral, seldom dark, and never black or white. . . ."

For one of his designs, Vaux recommends that the exterior be painted in quiet neutral tints, the main body of the work being a rather warm grey, while corner boards, verge boards, window dressings, verandah and porch are also of a greyish tint, but considerably darker than the other and with some brown added to it for sake of contrast. The stiles of the blinds should be rather lighter than the window dressings while the slats and the panels of the verge boards are a cool dark brown. The chimney would then be painted in tints to correspond. For another design, he says that the most harmonious arrangement of colors would be a soft reddish brick and a brownstone of as grey a tint as could be obtained. The roofs are then tinted a greenish grey and the eaves, verandah and other outside woodwork painted a warm oak color.

M. Field, in his *Rural Architecture* (New York, 1857), delivers an extensive essay on color in which he attacks white for destroying "graduations of distance."

This most glaring and disagreeable, but unfortunately most prevalent of colors, therefore, should be entirely eschewed, and light and neutral shades of gray, yellow or brown ochre substituted; which, with whiting, (or white lead) charcoal, bistre, and soot, are among the cheapest of colors and will produce any shade required. The brown sandstone tint often used, is generally too dark for the . . . distinction of the building from the trees. Bright green for blinds, fences, etc., is a color that ought to be avoided, as possessing neither contrast nor harmony with the natural color of foliage. A light or dark oak color, or a light leaden hue, would be far preferable. The best colors for gates and palings, would be the natural greenish grey, which they would acquire in time if left unpainted.

Much evidence exists that the bright green that Downing and his followers so violently objected to was a universally common trim color in the first years of the nineteenth century, despite the fact that James Gallier's *American Builder's General Price Book and Estimator* (New York, 1833) lists "good green" as the most expensive color, costing twice as much as the next lower color in price. Examples may be found in the tinted plates of:

1. C. A. Busby, *Collection of Designs for Modern Embellishments* (London, 1808).
2. Edmund Aitken, *Rural Buildings* (London, 1810).
3. J. B. Papworth, *Designs for Rural Residences* (London, 1818).
4. J. Thomson, *Retreats* (London, 1827).
5. Robert Lugar, *Villa Architecture* (London, 1828).
6. Francis B. Goodwin, *Domestic Architecture* (London, 1835).
7. Victor Petit, *Maisons de Campagne des Environs de Paris* (Paris, 1850).
8. Leon Isabey and Leblan, *Villas, Maisons de Ville et de Campagne* (Paris, 1864).
9. Victor Petit, *Habitations Cosmopolites* (Paris, 1867).
10. John Riddell, *Architectural Designs for Model Country Residences* (Philadelphia, 1864).

Samuel Sloan, a mid-century Philadelphia architect of considerable prominence, wrote several books and briefly published the *Architectural Review and American Builder's Journal*. Several of his works were advertised as having color plates, but, regretfully, the color work is too wan to have any educational value. His *The Model Architect* (Philadelphia,

1852), had three color plates: one of Bartram Hall, a Norman Villa designed for A. M. Eastwick, one of a grapery, and one of a suggested scheme for "picking out" a ceiling already much decorated with ornamental plasterwork. Of much greater value in terms of color are Sloan's specifications for the different designs. For one, he calls for painting and "sanding" the exterior walls in the best style. "Paint all exterior woodwork with four coats tinted and worked in imitation of old oak." For another, he says, "all exterior woodwork except the floors must either be painted and grained in imitation of oak or imitation of stone and sanded as may be directed." Elsewhere he recommends that "the doors and window frames externally must be tinted and grained to represent old oak and have two coats of varnish. The hood moulds and sills must be tinted and sanded to represent stone." Finally, in yet another design, he specifies, "all cornices, barges, window frames and sash, balconies and verandahs are to be painted in imitation of old oak. The head mouldings and corbels should be painted and sanded to represent stone." Earlier references to grained exterior woodwork and doors and windows may be found in:

1. Pierre de la Mesangere, *Meubles et Objets de Goût* (Paris, 1801-1835).
2. J. Thomson, *Retreats* (London, 1827).
3. Francis B. Goodwin, *Domestic Architecture* (London, 1835).

From the earliest years of the century, architects' drawings both here and abroad show grained exterior doors even where all other trim is painted. Graining and marbling also had universal application in the interiors of nineteenth century buildings of all economic classes both public and private. A cottage owner might use graining because its variegated color would tend to hide surface soil, just as its smooth varnished surface would allow for easier cleaning than the porous paint surfaces of the day. The landlord of a rental property would use graining because the above qualities would allow a painted surface to provide a long period of service without costly redecoration. In a more pretentious house, graining might be used as a substitute for costly cabinet woods or marbles otherwise beyond the budget of the builder. In a costly mansion, wood and marble graining was frequently used by "fresco" (i.e., interior decorative) painters as part of their elaborate schemes, even though the costly materials themselves could well be afforded by the builder or owner.

Another ornamental use of paint is specified by John Riddell in his *Architectural Designs for Model Country Residences* (Philadelphia, 1864). He calls for the porch roofs of several of his designs to be painted with awning stripes. (In one instance he recommends the same treatment for porch floors!) The color plates of his designs show striped porch roofs even on those houses whose specifications do not require them. That this practice was fashionable and followed by others than Riddell is supported by the photo-lithographed plates of A. A. Turner's *Villas on the Hudson* (New York, 1860), where three villas are shown with porch roofs painted in awning stripes. From a close examination of several John Notman houses, it is also believed that he used such stripes on his porches; the balcony roof of 1847 at The Athenaeum of Philadelphia is being so restored.

As late as 1866, Henry Hudson Holly still felt it necessary to argue against white and for "any of the hundred soft, neutral tints," but taste was beginning to swing against even these bland exterior color schemes. E. C. Hussey wrote in 1874, "painting is a matter of protection chiefly, but is of most vital importance also in regard to the beauty of a house; there is rarely an exception where a bright lively color is not far preferable. Avoid giving your house the *blues* or the *greens* with paint."

It is Holly, in his *Modern Dwellings* (New York, 1878) who offers us the case for the richer, darker color range that would dominate the last quarter of the century.

In cities, where the great value of land almost precludes the designer from availing himself of these opposing masses, which can be produced in emphasis only by costly irregularities of plan, and large re-entering angles of outer walls, it seems necessary to resort to some other expedient. . . . It would be well for us to take a lesson from the Eastern nations in this respect, and . . . study their picturesque use of external colors, and let the walls of our cities assume new life and meaning by contrasting tints of various bricks, stones, and brilliant tiles. . . .

I would not have it supposed that positive colors cannot be . . . [used] on the exteriors of country houses . . . green as the color for the blinds . . . has a cool and cheerful effect. . . . Still, if neutral tints are used on the body of the house, green is apt to appear too violent contrast unless a hue of some other harmonizing color be interposed. If the general tone of the house is drab or olive, a line of Indian red between this and the blinds would produce a relief. . . . I lay particular stress on the architect's directing the arrangement of the colors, as so many buildings are utterly spoiled by this important branch being taken out of his hands and intrusted to the mercies of the painter. Many of them are color blind. . . .

(Strong words, these!)

Upon any portion of the house receding from the façade, such as an alcoved balcony or recessed door-way, when deeply sunken, positive colors would be in keeping . . . [when an] exterior is of neutral buff, the sides of . . . [a deep window recess] are painted a deep ultramarine green; the trimmings of Indian red are relieved by lines of black and the coved ceiling is of brilliant blue.

F. B. Gardner says in *Everybody's Paint Book* (New York, 1884), that there is no reason why a house should be painted in the orthodox style of white with green blinds, or in drab colors with darker trimmings, but that it is now proper to launch out into dark green, black, red, etc., on city buildings. He cites that dark green made by mixing yellow and black may be made to look well with trimmings of black or gold; however, dwellings in villages or towns could not be thus darkened in color and should rather be painted tints of light or dark green, drab, buff, or salmon color which would prove, in most cases, superior to the monotonous white.

The March, 1894, issue of *Carpentry and Building* tells us:

The best paint is generally considered to be pure white lead mixed with oil and turpentine, color being added if desired. . . . Zinc white is another excellent paint, but it cannot be used by itself for exterior painting, as it is too hard and brittle and will easily scale and chip.

A large house was formerly painted in two tints of cold grey with yellow and red in large patches. A new owner employed warm browns and reds introducing into some of the mouldings "a little very bright brown and very bright red." A cheerless house was now most attractive. "A small house with a pitched roof might be painted as follows: siding up to first floor, a bright chocolate brown; siding above, very light sienna brown; trim, a brown darker than the lower part of the siding and with a little more red in it; shutters, a lighter tint of the same color; brick work in the foundations, red; roof, a reddish brown that has the appearance of having been made by mixing the chocolate brown on the lower clapboards with the red of the roof. When a light olive is used for the siding darker shades of the same color for the trim usually produce a good appearance."

Painters' colors had been offered in Boston early in the eighteenth century, and in 1754, in New York City, William Post founded the business that was to become Devoe, Reynolds & Company in the nineteenth century. Post ground earth powders and white lead and mixed them with oil using a crude stone mill; thereby establishing what is today one of the twenty oldest continuously operated businesses in the United States. White lead, however, appears to have been first manufactured in Philadelphia in 1804 by Samuel Wetherill. Soon thereafter, establishments were started in New York City, Boston and Pittsburgh. In the first quarter of the nineteenth century, the first commercial turpentine distillery was built in North Carolina, and production of linseed oil began to increase in all areas.

Despite this large scale commercial activity, the journeyman painter through the third quarter of the nineteenth century might or might not buy his white lead already mixed with oil, but almost invariably he purchased dry colors and mixed his own tinting combinations with a muller and slab, as had been done for centuries. White lead, if purchased as a dry powder, had to be thoroughly mixed with oil to provide the base for almost all paint. Laborious indeed were the common methods of obtaining this mix. One involved the use of an "eighty gallon or so stone trough" in which a two foot diameter stone ball would be rolled back and forth through a mass of dry white lead and a quantity of oil. As late as 1870, another method placed quantities of dry white lead and linseed oil in a large iron pot which was suspended on three chains. Two large iron balls were placed in this pot and a workman would seize the chains and rotate the pot. This set the balls to moving amid the mass of powder and oil, the process being maintained until the mass was sufficiently mixed for use, and, incidentally, long after the workman's hands were well blistered.

Complaints concerning debased white lead were legion and constant; the most common dilutant being ordinary whiting. A. J. Downing claimed in 1847 that four fifths of the white paint sold as "pure" white lead was actually composed largely of whiting. The poisonous effects of white lead were early recognized and the use of zinc white or zinc oxide suggested as an alternate. The use of zinc oxide was greatly inhibited by rather more expensive production, the fact that it was more difficult to brush out, did not cover as well, and was slower to dry. Despite its potential in the possible elimination of the harmful effects of white lead, zinc white never did assume its full potential as a paint pigment.

The practice of priming all exterior woodwork on a building with ochre ground-in-oil began with the fashion for more concentrated exterior colors and continued to World War I. By the 1890s, the practice had become so widespread that it was frequently given as a requirement in architect's specifications. *Carpentry and Building* for February, 1894, says, "perhaps the best primer is one composed of very finely ground yellow ochre; this is comparatively cheap, and answers the purpose admirably." This ochre priming is responsible for the exterior paint failure on most buildings of the late nineteenth and early twentieth centuries, as eighty years or more of drying has completely evaporated any oil from the primer, leaving only a layer of clay dust between the wood and the remaining paint film.

Five American paint manufacturers exhibited at the Crystal Palace in 1851, where records indicate that the display of the Wetherill firm was the largest and most comprehensive, including: anthracite coal, pure dry white lead, pure dry red lead, pure dry orange mineral, pure dry chrome yellow, twenty varieties of chemicals and pure ground white lead. Packaged paints were introduced about 1858, and were as often debased as "pure" white lead had been before them. As the Devoe Company explained in the original introduction to *Exterior Decoration,* the change in taste that required darker colors and, consequently, paints that were made up almost entirely of what had formerly been only tinting agents for white lead, required a whole new chemical composition and the use of processes that frequently were beyond the capabilities of the journeyman or the small paint shop.

Ready-mixed paint for general use was very slow in finding acceptance, despite the long, ardous, and messy labor involved in preparing materials in the painter's establishment or on the job. By the 1870s, however, ready-mixed paints prepared by reliable firms were becoming respectable, and the paint manufacturers were becoming prosperous enough to publish color cards with chips of actual paint. In a few instances, they published hardbound books such as the Devoe Company's *Exterior Decoration* (1885), that not only discussed the theory of color and displayed color chips, but also were illustrated with chromo-lithographs to show just how a variety of color combinations would appear on different style houses.

As anyone in the interior design profession knows, the only way that two or more persons can be certain they are discussing the same color is to have a sample of it before them. What a boon the color cards which began to appear in the 1870s must have been to contemporaries—as they are to us today! A number of these color cards from the 1870s and 1880s are known and listed in the new bibliography of *Exterior Decoration.* One of the largest collection of color cards available in the United States today is at The Athenaeum of Philadelphia. In one such color book the publisher wrote, "the designs are, in themselves models of taste. Each building is shown decorated in two or three different styles. . . . The portfolio is intended to be loaned upon application, with a guarantee that it will be returned in good condition, or sold at $20.00." It would seem that paint books cost nearly as much in the 1880s as they do today.

Bibliography of Some Original Paint Sources

The most important sources for the study of mid-to-late nineteenth century paint colors are the illustrated catalogues and color cards of American ready-mixed paint manufacturers. The pioneering bibliography of business catalogues of all types is Lawrence B. Romaine, *A Guide to American Trade Catalogs, 1744-1900* (New York, 1960). Romaine lists over thirty of these for paint, but omits many of the most important. The following bibliography includes his listings and those additional discoveries now in The Athenaeum of Philadelphia and Victorian Society collections and the large trade catalogue holdings of the Eleutherian Mills Hagley Foundation Library. It is hoped that anyone knowing of other catalogues and color cards will bring them to the attention of the research staff at The Athenaeum.

Acme White Lead & Color Works,
When your house is painted; things to think of by the painter and the one who pays the bill (Detroit, c. 1900), 12 p., illus. Location: DeWE.
Alexander's,
Romaine lists a sixteen page illustrated catalogue of Alexander's Four Ace paints (Chicago, 1864). Location: IHi.
Allentown Manufacturing Company,
Breinig's ready mixed pure linseed oil paints (Allentown, Pa., c. 1890), 14 p., color chips. Locations: DeWE and PHi.

Averill & Company,
Romaine lists an early unillustrated catalogue of Averill's paint for tin roofs, bridges, steamboats, railroad cars and buildings (Newburgh, Ohio, c. 1865). Location: OHi.

Chicago White Lead & Oil Company,
Romaine lists an illustrated price list (Chicago, 1888-9). Location: MnHi.

————.
"Samples of 'The King' Tinted Paint," 48 color chips bound into *The National Builder Supplement* (Chicago, 1887) V, 6. Location: PPAth (VSA).

Devoe, F. W. & Company,
Exterior decoration (New York, 1885), 95 p., 20 color plates, fifty color chips. The basis for this book, four copies of *Exterior Decoration* are known: a copy in The Victorian Society Collection at PPAth, two others at DeNU and DeWE, and a privately owned copy.

————.
Devoe velour finish and mottletone effects (New York, n.d.). Location: DeWE.

————.
Manufacturers and importers of colors, dry and ground in oil, white lead, zinc white, artist's materials and varnishes (New York, c. 1883), 135 p., color illus. Location: DeWE.

Egyptian Lacquer Manufacturing Company,
Romaine lists a sixty page illustrated catalogue of transparent and colored lacquers (New York, 1896). Location: NNMM.

Felton, Sibley & Company,
Romaine lists a folding color card of ready-mixed paints for buggy, carriage, and sleigh (Philadelphia, c. 1890). Location: DeWE.

Gibsboro Color Varnish Company,
Romaine lists this twenty four page price list and color card distributed by John Lucas & Company (Gibsboro, New Jersey, 1887). Location: NjR.

Harrison Brothers and Company,
The Chemistry of paints, or, a partial description of the Harrison white lead, color and chemical works, with a practical treatise on painting (Philadelphia, c. 1890), 41 p., illustrated. Location: DeWE.

————.
Colors of ready mixed roof paints ("These paints may be used on fences, barns and other work.") (Philadelphia, c. 1890), card with color chips. Location: DeWE.

————.
Descriptive catalogue and price list. (Philadelphia, c. 1898), 96 p., illustrated. Location: DeWE (also a price list of 1893).

————.
Special jobber's list, "Harrisons" strictly pure oil colors (Philadelphia, 1886), broadside. Location: DeWE.

Heath & Milligan Manufacturing Company,
Best prepared paints ready for use (Chicago, c. 1890), 42 p., 20 color plates. Location: PPAth.

Johns, H. W. Manufacturing Company,
H. W. Johns patent asbestos materials (New York, c. 1878), 48 p. Location: PPAth.

————.
H. W. Johns patent asbestos materials (New York, 1881), 48 p., 32 color chips. "In 1858 we commenced the manufacture of Compositions, Coatings and Paints for preserving wood, metals, fabrics, etc. . . . In 1868 we first made known the results of our . . . experiments with Asbestos. . . . In 1874 we commenced the manufacture . . . of Liquid Paints." Location: PPAth.

————.
"Asbestos Liquid Paints," 40 color chips bound into Robert W. Shoppell, *How to build, furnish and decorate* (New York, 1883). Location: PPAth (VSA).

————.
Structural decoration (New York, 1884), 48 p., 2 pages of color samples. Especially interesting are the wood engravings of structures painted with H. W. Johns's paints, keyed by name and number to the color chips in the 1881 catalogue listed above. The two catalogues should be consulted together. Location: PPAth.

————.
Artistic house painting (New York, 1895), 20 p., 7 color plates. Location: PPAth.

————.
Romaine lists two twelve page illustrated catalogues with color samples for 1896 and 1897. Location: MH-BA.

Lehigh Coal and Hardware Company,
Breinig's ready-mixed pure linseed oil paints (Leighton, Pa., c. 1890), 5 p., color samples. Location: DeWE.

Longman & Martinez,
Romaine lists a nineteen page illustrated catalogue and price list of colors, oils, varnishes and paints with color chips (Brooklyn, New York, 1885). Location: NNQ.

Lucas, John & Company,

John Lucas & Co., established 1849; proprietors of the Gibbsboro Paint, Color & Varnish Works (Philadelphia, c. 1870?), 24 p., illus., 3 color chips. Location: DeWE.

———.

For roofing, seashore, railway, and house painting, barn, bridge, and building ready mixed paint (Philadelphia, 1890), 4 p., color chips. Location: DeWE.

———.

Portfolio of modern house painting designs (Philadelphia, 1887). This is by far the most spectacular of the display books discovered to date. It contains twenty-four large (19″ x 24″) color plates "to offer greater variety in the selection of colors." The Lucas Company claimed that "a departure in the past ten years or more from the conventional styles of architecture peculiar to this country has led to a more cultivated taste in the use of colors, both for interior and exterior decoration, and whilst we may see occasionally what can best be described as an abortion in the attempt to produce a sensation, the dissemination of a more perfect knowledge of the effect of colors in combination and the increasing demand for more tasteful display in this respect is one of the most pleasing signs of the march of improvement and increasing refinement of the American people." Location: PPAth (VSA).

———.

Romaine lists two 1870 catalogues of eleven and twenty-seven pages respectively containing color charts (locations: PHi and DeWE), and a 1878 price list with color samples. Location: PHi.

Masury & Whiton; John W. Masury & Son,

Romaine lists a thirty-two page catalogue of railroad colors with samples, c. 1870 (location MH-BA); a twenty-four page catalogue of 1871 (location: NSbSM); another for 1872 (NSbSM); and a sample book for carriage, coach and car work of eleven plates, c. 1875 (NNMM). The Athenaeum owns a John W. Masury & Son *Net price list for 1881* (New York, 1881), 12 p.

Moller & Schumann,

Romaine lists catalogues of 1880 and 1881 for this Watson, New York, firm. Location: NNQ.

Moore, Benjamin & Company,

Muresco tints for wall & ceiling decoration (New York and Chicago, c. 1905), single folded sheet with 14 color chips. Location: PPAth.

Moser, Charles & Company,

Romaine lists an undated catalogue containing twenty leaves of color illustrations by this Cincinnati firm. Location: NNMM.

New York Enamel Paint Company,

Sample color card (New York, c. 1900), single folded sheet with 30 color chips. Location: PPAth.

Noyes Brothers & Cutler,

Romaine lists this illustrated fifty-two page catalogue of brushes, oils, paints and varnishes (St. Paul, Minn., 1888). Location: MnHi.

Pierce, F. O. & Company,

Romaine lists this major illustrated catalogue of thirty-one leaves with twenty-four color plates similar to the Heath, Johns, and Wetherill catalogues listed here (New York, c. 1884). Location: NNMM.

Pittsburg Plate Glass Company,

Catalogue A: glass, paints, oils and painters' sundries (Philadelphia, c. 1901), 254 p., 32 plates in color. Locations: PPAth and NNMM.

Raynolds, C. T. and Company,

Sample book and price list of quick drying coach colors, ground in Japan & gold size (New York, 1887), 33 p., illus., color chips. Location: DeWE.

Sears, Roebuck and Company,

S. R. & Co's paints (Chicago, c. 1895), 12 p., illus., color chips. Location: DeWE.

Seeley Brothers,

Averill Paint . . . (N. Y., c. 1880), 20 color plates, 39 color chips, 2 ads in color (one for "Alabastine" with 12 color chips). Locations: DeWWin and NNMM.

Senour Manufacturing Company,

Monarch mixed paint (Chicago, c. 1885), 8 p., 48 color chips. Location: PPAth.

———.

Supplement to our regular monarch color card of forty-eight shades (Chicago, c. 1888), 16 p., 16 color chips. "This Card Represents twelve of the most popular House Colors taken from our Regular Monarch Card. Also four trimming colors for Window Blinds, Sash and Doors." Location: PPAth.

———.

Senour's ornamental paints (Chicago, c. 1885), 4 p., 20 color chips. Location: PPAth.

Sherwin-Williams Company,

Catalogue of paints and colors for railway use (Cleveland, Ohio, c. 1885). This extraordinary book contains 172 pages, folding plans, ten color plates and 108 color chips. While intended for the railroad trade (the plates show rolling stock and station buildings), the color range is typical of residential house paints in the 1880s and 1890s. Location: PPAth.

Shoemaker, Robert and Company,
   Romaine lists this forty page illustrated catalogue of brushes, oils, paints and varnishes. (Philadelphia, 1867.) Location: PHi.

Tiemann, D. F. & Company,
   D. F. Tiemann & Co., manufacturers of the celebrated brands of Tiemann's Colors, dry & ground in oil and water; varnishes, &c. importers of and dealers in zinc white, white lead and paints (New York, 1859), 24 p. Location: DeWE.

Valentine & Company,
   Romaine lists this forty page illustrated catalogue with color chips for coach and railroad car varnishes and paints (New York, 1889). Location: TxDaDeG.

Vieille Montagne Zinc Mining Company,
   Explanatory notice of the patent French, Belgian, and Silesian white oxide of zinc and instructions for its use as a paint (New York, 1856), 20 p. Location: DeWE.

Wadsworth, Martinez & Longman,
   Romaine lists this twenty page catalogue containing eight color illustrations of "homes and buildings in various combinations of *garish* colors" [emphasis added]. (Brooklyn, N. Y., 1882). Location: NNQ.

Wetherill, George D. & Company,
   Painters' and builders' hand-book: suggestions in house painting and coloring (Philadelphia, 1886), 11 color plates (6″ x 9″) and a color card of 36 chips. (Wetherill claimed to have published a *Portfolio of artistic designs* in 1884, consisting of twenty-seven "elaborately colored engravings of hotels, dwellings, churches, stables, etc." No complete copy of the Wetherill *Portfolio* has been discovered. What appears to be an incomplete copy containing twenty-two of twenty-seven large color plates is listed among the holdings of DeWE.) Location: PPAth.

Wilhelm Company,
   Dealer's reference book (Reading, Pa., c. 1900), 78 p., illus. Location: DeWE.

Ziegler & Smith,
   Romaine lists this illustrated fifty page catalogue of white leads, zincs, colors, putty and supplies. Contains color plates of stained glass windows (Philadelphia, 1873). Location: NNMM (Similar catalogues for 1872 and 1874 at PHi).

List of Location Symbols

DeWE	Eleutherian Mills Hagley Foundation, Wilmington, Delaware
DeWWin	Winterthur Museum, Winterthur, Delaware
DeNU	University of Delaware Library, Newark, Delaware
IHi	Illinois State Historical Library, Springfield, Illinois
MH-BA	Harvard University—Baker Library, Cambridge, Massachusetts
MnHi	Minnesota Historical Society, St. Paul, Minnesota
NjR	Rutgers University Library, New Brunswick, New Jersey
NNMM	Metropolitan Museum of Art, New York, New York
NNQ	Queensborough Public Library, New York, New York
NSbSM	Suffolk Museum, Stony Brook, New York
OHi	Ohio Historical Society, Columbus, Ohio
PHi	Historical Society of Pennsylvania,
PPAth	Athenaeum of Philadelphia, Philadelphia, Pennsylvania
PPAth (VSA)	Victorian Society in America, Athenaeum of Philadelphia
TxDaDeG	DeGolyer Foundation, Dallas, Texas

Select Bibliography

The following works were consulted in the preparation of the introduction. Several useful bibliographies have been compiled that the serious student would want to consult for the history and technology of paint prior to c. 1820 and after c. 1900. The most extensive of these is by John Volz, "Paint Bibliography," *Newsletter* of The Association for Preservation Technology (February, 1975), which gives over four hundred and fifty entries. Also, see Theodore Zuk Penn, "Decorative and Protective Finishes, 1750-1850: Materials, Process, and Craft," (Unpublished thesis University of Delaware, 1966).

Aitken, Edmund. *Rural Buildings*. London, 1810.

Allen, Edward B. *Early American Wall Paintings,* New Haven, 1926.

Allen, Lewis F. *Rural Architecture*. New York, 1860.

Arnot, D. H. *Gothic Architecture Applied to Modern Residences*. New York, 1851.

Arrowsmith, H. W. and A. *The House Decorator and Painter's Guide*. London, 1840.

Arrowsmith, James. *The Paper-Hanger's Companion*. Philadelphia, 1852.

Atwood, Daniel. *Country and Suburban Houses*. New York, 1871.

Audsley, W. & G. *Cottage, Lodge and Villa Architecture*. London, n.d., c. 1860.

———. *Polychromatic Decoration*. London, 1882.

Babbitt, Edwin S. *The Principles of Light and Color*. New York, 1967.

Baird, Henry Carey. *The Painter, Gilder, and Varnisher's Companion*. Philadelphia, 1854.

Banov, Abel. *Paints & Coatings Handbook*. Farmington, Mich., 1973.

Birren, Faber. *Munsell-A Grammar of Color*. New York, 1969.

Boyce, Allen P. *Boyce's Modern Ornamentor and Interior Decorator*. Boston, 1874.

Brannt, William T. *The Painter, Gilder & Varnisher's Companion* (27th edition, Philadelphia, 1894, see Baird above).

Brown, Richard. *Domestic Architecture*. London, 1842.

Brown, William Norman. *House Decorating and Painting*. London, 1900.

Brunner, A. W. (ed.). *Cottages or Hints on Economical Building*. New York, 1884.

Butcher, William. *Smith's Art of House-Painting Improved by Wm. Butcher* (3rd edition, London, 1857).

Bullock, John. *The American Cottage Builder*. New York, 1854.

Busby, C. A. *Collection of Designs for Modern Embellishments*. London, 1808.

Cawse, J. *Introduction to the Art of Painting in Oil Colours*. London, 1829.

Chevreul, Michel E. *The Laws of Contrast of Colour, and their application to the Arts*. (London, 1857).

Church, A. H. *The Chemistry of Paints and Painting*. London, 1890.

Clay, R. M. "From Blue Lead to White Lead," *Country Life* (June 30, 1950).

Cleaveland, Henry W. and William and Samuel D. Backus. *Village and Farm Cottages*. New York, 1856.

Clouzot, Henri. *Des Tuileries à Saint-Cloud*. Paris, 1925.

Condit, Charles L. *Painting and Painters' Materials*. New York, 1883.

Cook, Clarence. *The House Beautiful*. New York, 1878.

———. *What Shall We Do With Our Walls?* New York, 1880.

Croft-Murray, Edward. *Decorative Painting in England, 1537-1837*. (London, 1970).

Curtis, George W. *The Potiphar Papers*. New York, 1856.

Daly, Cesare. *L'Architecture Privée au XIXe Siècle*. Paris, 1877. 3rd. Ser.

Davey, Norman. *A History of Building Materials*. New York, 1971.

Davidson, Ellis A. *A Practical Manual of House-Painting, Graining, Marbling and Sign Writing*. London, third edition, 1880.

Devoe, Raynolds & Company. *Our 200th Anniversary Report*. New York, 1954.

Dicks, John (publisher). *The Illustrated Carpenter & Builder*. London, 1883.

Downing, A. J. *The Architecture of Country Houses*. New York, 1850.

———. *Cottage Residences*. New York, 1844.

Downs, Arthur C., Jr. "The Introduction of American Zinc Paints, ca. 1850," *Bulletin* of The Association of Preservation Technology (1974), VI, 36-37.

Dresser, Christopher. *Principles of Decorative Design*. London, 1873.

Durenne, A. *Fonte de Fer*. Paris, n.d., c. 1860.

Dwyer, Charles P. *The Economic Cottage Builder*. Buffalo, 1855.

Eastlake, Charles L. *Hints on Household Taste*. Boston, fourth American edition, 1876.

Edis, Robert. *Decoration and Furniture of Town Houses*. London, 1881.

Elliott, Charles Wyllys. *The Book of American Interiors*. Boston, 1876.

Ellis, Robert (ed.). *Official Descriptive and Illustrated Catalogue, Great Exhibition of the Works of Industry of All Nations, 1851*. London, 1851.

Every Man His Own Painter! or, Paints—How to Select and Use Them. Philadelphia, 1873.

Field, George and E. A. Davidson. *A Grammar of Colouring Applied to Decorative Arts*. London, 1875.

———. *The Rudiments of Colours and of Colouring*. London, 1870.

———. *Rudiments of the Painters' Art*. London, 1858.

Field, M. *Rural Architecture*. New York, 1857.

Fowler, Orson S. *A Home For All*. New York, 1854.

Gallier, James. *The American Builder's General Price Book and Estimator*. New York, 1833.

Gardner, Franklin B. *Everybody's Paint Book*. New York, 1884.

Garnier, Charles. *Le Nouvel Opéra de Paris*. Paris, 1880-1881.

Garnsey, George O. (ed.). *The National Builder*. Chicago, 1885-1888.

Garrett, Rhoda and Agees. *Suggestions for House Decoration in Painting, Woodwork, and Furniture*. Philadelphia, 1877.

Goodwin, Francis B. *Domestic Architecture*. London, 1835.

Graef, F. *The House, a Pocket Manual*. New York, 1859.

Grinnell, V. B. *Grinnell's Handbook of Painting*. Vinton, Iowa, 1894.

Harris, Moses. *The Natural System of Colours* (1766). New York, reprinted, 1963.

Harrison, W. R. *Practical Guide to Decorative Painting for Walls, Panels, Screens, and Terra-cotta*. London, 1883.

Housepainting and Decorating. Philadelphia, 1885-1890.

Harley, R. D. *Artist's Pigments, c. 1600-1835*. New York, 1970.

Hay, D. R. *The Laws of Harmonious Coloring*. London, fourth edition, 1838.

Higgins, W. Mullinger. *The House Painter; or, Decorator's Companion.* London, 1841.

Holly, Henry Hudson. *Country Seats.* New York, 1866.

———. *Modern Dwellings.* New York, 1878.

Hurst, George Henry. *Painters' Colours, Oils, and Varnishes: A Practical Manual.* London, 1892.

Hussey, E. C. *Hussey's National Cottage Architecture.* New York, 1874.

Isabey, Leon. *Villas, Maisons de Ville et de Campagne.* Paris, 1864.

Jones, Mrs. C. S. and Henry T. Williams. *Beautiful Homes and How to Make Them.* Rockford, Ill., 1885.

Jourdain, Margaret. *English Interior Decoration, 1500-1830.* London, 1950.

Linfoot, Ben (ed.). *The American Architect and Builders' Monthly.* Philadelphia, 1870-1871.

Little, Nina Fletcher. *American Decorative Wall Painting, 1700-1850.* Sturbridge, Mass., 1952.

Loudon, J. C. *An Encyclopaedia of Cottage, Farm and Villa Architecture.* London, 1835.

Lowe Brothers Company. *The House Outside and Inside: How to Make Your Home Attractive.* Dayton, Ohio, 1914.

Lugar, Robert. *Villa Architecture.* London, 1828.

McDannell, D. S. *The Practical Painter and Instructor.* Chicago, 1874.

McLean, R. C. (ed.). *The Inland Architect and Builder.* Chicago, 1883.

Masury, John W. *The American Grainer's Handbook.* New York, 1872.

———. *How Shall We Paint Our Houses?* New York, 1868.

Mesangere, Pierre de la. *Meubles, et Objets de Goût* Supplement to *Journal des Dames et des Modes.* Paris 1801-1835.

Mitchell, F. Scott. *A Few Suggestions for Ornamental Decoration.* London, 1908.

Moore, G. B. *The Principles of Colour Applied to Decorative Art.* London, 1851.

Neil, J. W. *The Painters Guide to the Art of Varnishing and Polishing.* London, 1824.

Papworth, J. B. *Designs for Rural Residences.* London, 1818.

Patmore, Derek. *Colour Schemes for the Modern Home.* London, 1933.

Peterson, Charles E. "Early Sanded Paint Finish," *Journal* of The Society of Architectural Historians (October, 1950), IX,3.

Petit, Victor. *Habitations Cosmopolites.* Paris, 1867.

———. *Maisons de Campagne des Environs de Paris.* Paris, n.d., c. 1850.

Putnam, G. P. *Official Catalogue of the New York Exhibition of the Industry of All Nations.* New York, 1853.

Ranlett, William H. *The Architect.* New York, 1854.

Reed, S. B. *House-plans for Everybody.* New York, 1882.

Riddell, John. *Architectural Designs for Model Country Residences.* Philadelphia, 1864.

Ritch, John W. *The American Architect.* New York, n.d., c. 1847.

Rossiter, E. K. and F. A. Wright. *Modern House Painting.* New York, 1883.

Seldon, Marjorie Ward. *The Interior Paint of the Campbell-Whittlesey House, 1835-1836.* Rochester, New York, 1949.

Seward, B. C. *Decorative Painting, a Practical Handbook.* London, 1883.

Shaw, Edward. *Shaw's Civil Architecture.* Boston, 1852.

Shoppell, Robert W. *Builders' Portfolio.* New York, 1883.

———. *A Choice Collection, Shoppell's Modern Houses.* New York, 1895.

———. *How to Build, Furnish and Decorate.* New York, 1883.

Sloan, Samuel. *American Houses.* Philadelphia, 1861.

———. *City and Suburban Architecture.* Philadelphia, 1861.

———. *Homestead Architecture.* Philadelphia, 1861.

———. *Model Architect.* Philadelphia, 1860.

———. *Sloan's Constructive Architecture.* Philadelphia, 1859.

Spofford, Harriet P. *Art Decoration Applied to Furniture.* New York, 1878.

Stokes, J. *The Cabinet-maker and Upholsterer's Companion.* Philadelphia, 1858.

Tingry, Pierre-François. *Painter's and Colourman's Complete Guide.* London, 1830.

Thomson, J. *Retreats.* London, 1827.

Turner, A. A. *Villas on the Hudson.* New York, 1860.

Vanherman, T. H. *Every Man His Own House-Painter and Colourman.* London, 1829.

Varney, Almon C. *Our Homes and Their Adornments.* Detroit, 1883.

Vaux, Calvert. *Villas and Cottages.* New York, 1857.

Wall, William Edmund. *Graining Ancient and Modern.* Somerville, Mass., 1905.

———. *Practical Graining with Description of Colors Employed and Tools Used.* Philadelphia, 1891.

Wheeler, Candace. *Principles of Home Decoration.* New York, 1908.

Wheeler, Gervase. *Homes for the People.* New York, 1855.

———. *Rural Homes.* New York, 1851.

Whittock, Nathaniel. *The Decorative Painters' and Glaziers' Guide.* London, 1828.

Wickes, Charles. *A Handy Book on Villa Architecture.* London, 1862.

Wightwick, George and A. J. Downing. *Hints to Young Architects.* New York, 1847.

Wilkinson, J. Gardner. *On Colour.* London, 1858.

Williams, David (ed.). *Carpentry and Building.* New York, 1894.

Woodward, George E. *Woodward's National Architect.* New York, 1869.

PREFATORY.

In preparing what is intended to be a concise treatise on the exterior painting and decoration of the modern dwelling, the object the publishers have sought to attain has been, primarily, to familiarize the public, as far as this is possible in a few brief pages, with the true principles of correct and tasteful coloring as applied to this class of work. Practical teachings on such a subject, even where available to the fullest extent, do not suffice where the best results are sought; theory on the other hand cannot be exclusively relied upon; the painter must be something more than a mere manipulator of colors, while the artist must go outside of his school to find a means of utilizing his knowledge of the science of chromatics.

Practice, however, is essential to the profitable employment of theory, and the two combined constitute the basis of all success in the correct employment and grouping or arrangement of colors and the production of the most agreeable and harmonious decorative effects. The results of the scientist's study of light as reflected by different surfaces—color, as we are used to call it,—as representing the theory of chromatics, will be found in the following pages tempered with the artist's practical knowledge of effects, as governed by the varying surroundings, by architectural considerations, by modern tastes, requirements and predilections, as well as by the appreciation of the protective and preservative properties of paints that comes to the painter through practical observation of their durability, and to the chemist through a study of their character and constituents in his laboratory. Finally, we shall devote a brief space to the consideration of the value especially of such paints as modern tastes call for, from an economical standpoint and in the interest alike of manufacturers, dealers in and users of paints, adding a few practical hints concerning their selection and application and the durability of their materials under different conditions.

In short, our endeavor will be to condense, within a few brief pages, information that will be found of value either to the painter or to the person for or by whom paints are to be used, and who may be desirous of seeing them tastefully, efficiently and economically employed; and we shall also give, in the form of plates showing the effective and harmonious combination and contrast of colors under different conditions as to landscape, architecture, etc, some practical illustrations of the application of the principles of which we strive to impart a knowledge.

ART IN HOUSE PAINTING.

The earliest employment of paints, as far as can be learned from the relics of antiquity and the works of early authors on decoration, etc., recognized only their ornamental value, and we have no positive proof that colors or pigments of any kind were applied to buildings for protective purposes. Chemistry had not come to the painter's aid to supply him with materials possessing preservative properties, and the pigments he used for general decorative purposes mostly ochres, umbers, siennas and other simple preparations—were few in number, and used entirely with a view to the production of ornamental effect. Such, indeed, was the case for many subsequent ages, and only within the past two or three centuries have paints been employed for the purpose of obviating the effects of the atmosphere, moisture and their indigenous elements of decay, on such destructible bodies as are employed for constructive purposes.

At first, as soon as the preservative properties of oil paints were recognized and made known, a rapid increase in their employment took place, but their popularity was based almost exclusively on their protective value, their utility only was considered without regard to their appearance or effect, and they were applied indiscriminately to every size and style of building alike. Such have been the conditions that have prevailed to a great extent in the painter's art ever since, and at the present date these remarks are still very widely applicable. We find the same white houses with green blinds that our forefathers delighted in predominant now, no attempt in many instances having been made to render a building anything more than a glaringly prominent and unnatural feature amid its natural surroundings; and the harsh, cold contrast of a white or light shade of color with the quiet and subdued tones that for the most part prevail in our landscape, is yet everywhere noticeable. Theoretical artists, with their erroneous ideas of color; the house-owner, with his fond adherence to established precedent and tradition, however hideous it might be; and even the painter, in his inexperience of color effects, have all been to blame for the long perpetuation of these crude ideas, in which art, as representing tasteful effect, agreeable harmony and judicious contrast of color, was sacrificed entirely to utility, and their joint and similar opinions were maintained with steadfast pertinac-

ity. The change came very gradually, the white being at first tempered for the sake of variety with cold tints of grey, lavender, green, blue and other colors, totally unfit for the purpose they were intended to serve, but still of value as stepping-stones to better things; the rare examples of the use of deeper shades, of warm rich tints and a variety of colors in exterior decoration, were falsely spoken of as "loud," when really, compared with the old style of painting, their effect was subdued and restful. The new idea in painting, as it was termed, had, however, found friends, it was permanently before the world, and gradually the sole consideration of utility became tempered with a desire for artistic effect. The truest form of art is always that in which it is combined with utility, and our present method of successful house painting, the employment of colors capable of producing a really ornamental appearance, and at the same time protecting the material to which they are applied, embody both art and utility.

Two of the most important factors in thus developing artistic taste in exterior decoration have been, in the first place, the material our architects have largely had to deal with and the prevailing style of architecture. Wood not only needs painting to ensure its durability, but is capable, while serving every constructive purpose, of being wrought into the most picturesque effects. It is the material with which our modern architects have chiefly had to deal in the erection of dwellings, except within the limits of the largest cities, and they have been most successful in adapting it to the requirements of artistic ideas since the most popular type of architecture for our residence structure came into vogue; we refer to the Queen Anne style, as it is usually termed. To give the true origin of the Queen Anne architecture would be somewhat difficult, for in it are combined some of the features of the mediæval gothic, others pertaining to the renaissance of the Roman and Grecian classic styles, and many others that are probably derived from one style or another, but which have lost all but the barest traces of their origin. It has come to be regarded, in short, as the vehicle for the expression of almost everything quaint and uncommon in the shape of architecture, no particular style, it is true, if measured by the "school" standard, but a welcome change from the "ready made" architecture that preceded it, and which, in its bald bareness and abrupt quadrilateral and quadrangular features, displayed a fatiguing sameness that is still characteristic of most of our city streets and many of our country residences, and which the painter's art can alone be relied on to render even passably attractive.

The original Queen Anne style of dwelling was essentially a comfortable residence, it was designed according to the plan, the exterior appearance being subordinated to the interior arrangement. Such are the prevailing features in the specimens of early colonial architecture that are yet to be found scattered throughout the country, and although in subsequent years much detail, borrowed both from the gothic renaissance and the classical periods, was added, and special success attained in adapting the material to the architect's designs and our ideas of ornament, the purity of the Queen Anne style (if it really possessed any) was longest preserved in this country. The improvements to which we have referred paved the way for the modern Queen Anne style, now the favorite here, and deservedly so. In its embellished form it admits, without any appearance of incongruity, of the production of the quaintest effects both in the grouping of the parts of a building, the general appearance produced and the working out of the details in the shape of doors, windows, etc. It is, moreover, a form that admits of the most comfortable and attractive arrangement of the interior, and above all, and what most concerns us, it furnishes an opportunity for the greatest display of taste in coloring and exterior decoration. The many fronts, diversified as to material, with visible framing, shingle or smooth covering, the gables, the porches, etc., all provide a means for the employment of parti-colored effects, the most attractive and artistically valuable feature of modern house painting, and one that the old box-pattern house, with its plain flat front, does not so readily admit of.

Nor have we been slow to profit by the opportunity thus offered. The development, for such it really is, in architectural taste, the adaptation of the exterior form of our dwellings to the luxury and elegance of their interior arrangement and ornamentation, has been seconded within the past few years by equal care and the display of corresponding taste in color and decorative design, and in the production of that harmony combined with contrast between the various features in the house itself, and between the house and its surroundings, that underlies all true art. To-day, the architect, where he values his reputation and is desirous of giving his clients perfect satisfaction, is as solicitous of the color effect as of the general design of his work.

It must not be forgotten, however, that the majority of the buildings the painter is called on to embellish and render attractive, were erected before the present change or renaissance of the modern building art, came into force. They still preserve their plainness of exterior, their walls bare, except for windows and window-trim, etc., their flat roofs adorned at most with a chimney or cupola, and the old plan of treatment with white or light colors is still followed for want of a knowledge of what would suit their peculiar, unartistic style. They have been practically ignored in previous works on this subject, though so important a factor in the painter's operations, and yet their skilful treatment, the moderation of their harsh and unattractive characteristics, is to be regarded as the best possible evidence of artistic training on the part of the painter. To render such buildings ornamental, demands the exercise of the colorists's most careful discretion, and it will be found that we have not neglected this most important branch of our subject. We fully recognize, in fact, that to be successful, the painter, or the person directing the use of paints, should possess an equal knowledge with the architect and the artist of the laws governing the selection of colors, not only for the picturesque buildings of the style to which we have referred more particularly, on account of their present predominance, and for others equally attractive in the English-domestic, free-classic, colonial, gothic and other now popular styles, but for every structure, plain or ornamental, handsome or unattractive, on which paints are employed for decorative and protective purposes.

THE ARTISTIC SELECTION AND COMBINATION OF COLORS.

In the selection of the colors employed in the exterior decoration of buildings, we find the truest expression of the painter's artistic taste and skill; herein there are many factors to be studied, a disregard of any of which will be more or less fatal to good effect, and the first requisite is a knowledge of this art of associating the various colors in such a manner as to secure an agreeable contrast without doing violence to the harmony of the color group.

CHOICE OF COLORS WITH REGARD TO THEIR COMBINATION AND CONTRAST.

A brief reference to the classification of colors according to their value and effects as pigments, is essential to their proper employment and combination. The primary colors, those that cannot be produced from mixtures of other colors, and which in their turn are the basis of all color combinations, are red, yellow and blue. The secondary colors, green, orange and purple, are obtained by combinations of the primary colors—blue and yellow producing green; red and yellow, orange; and blue and red, purple. In the same manner, by mixtures of the secondary, we obtain the tertiary colors, orange and purple producing russet; green and purple, olive; green and orange, citrine. These nine constitute the normal or positive colors. White and black are regarded by most scientists as no colors at all, but combined they form gray, and these three, under the title of the neutral colors, are employed in lightening, darkening or dulling all other hues. Each of the positive colors, and all the immense variety of shades and tints derived from them, can be reduced with the aid of white, darkened by the use of black, or dulled by admixture with gray. Colors may harmonize in resemblance or by contrast, a harmony in resemblance being obtained by the employment of various shades and depths of the same color, a harmony by contrast consisting in the use of opposing colors, generally a neutral and a positive, a warm and a colder color. In the perfect contrast designed to effect an improvement in the colors employed, all the primary colors must be present either in simple or combined form, and the same rule applies to the secondary and tertiary colors, each of which harmonizes with its primary or secondary derivatives. Red and green for instance, contrast harmoniously, the red, with the blue and yellow of the green, making up the list of primary colors. Blue and orange, yellow and purple, also harmonize by contrast. By placing a dark by the side of a light color each will be intensified, the light appears lighter, the dark darker; if red and green be placed in contrast, though they will harmonize, the red will appear redder and the green greener. Much the same principle may be observed respecting harmony in resemblance, the light and dark shades of the same color increasing in intensity of difference when brought into juxtaposition. Blue is a cold color and appears to recede from the eye, hence the cold distant effect produced by a sky background. Red, on the contrary, is a warm color, it remains stationary in a picture, while yellow, the color nearest allied to light, has a brightening effect on its surroundings and appears to advance towards the observer. However carefully we may select colors with a view to their scientific harmony, we should make it a rule, wherever possible, to test the effects of every combination we propose to use at a distance and ascertain how its colors will appear under such different conditions as they are likely to be subject to. These rules embody about all that will be found essential to success in estimating the value and effect of colors and selecting them for combination, and they will prove particularly useful to the painter who regards his business as something beyond a merely mechanical pursuit.

In considering the effective value of the various colors and the best plan on which they can be artistically combined, we must make it a rule to set aside all considerations of surroundings, etc., for, if desirous of obtaining a perfect result, the colors must be studied independently and entirely *per se ;* the association of the colors and combinations with their various surroundings belonging in another chapter, and for the following reason: We have to deal, in selecting colors, with the cold scientific theory of chromatics. The building, however attractive its form, the surroundings, however picturesque they may be, are powerless to transform our bad judgment or improve on our defects in the combination of colors, for there is nothing, as there is in natural effects, that we can rely on to modify either. Blue and green, for instance, under any ordinary circumstances, and for decorative purposes, could not be regarded as an agreeable or harmonious contrast in color, and yet we find in nature, in the juxtaposition of green trees with the blue background of sky, just such a combination. But it will be found on close examination, that the green of the foliage has been transformed by the bright sunlight into a green yellow at all prominent points, or it is shaded and presents a greyish green or brownish green appearance; so that we have either of the latter warm colors with the blue of the sky, and they constitute an excellent contrast. We should rather look upon our house as a piece of coloring, intended, like a flower, to relieve the sameness in nature's prevailing hues, and, like the flower, it should be in itself a perfect piece of coloring

In the first place, our colors must not be violently opposed to each other, and here the eye may in most cases be safely left to discriminate. While the contrast in color should be sufficient to relieve the large expanse of uniform tint inseparable from the tasteful decoration of any house, especially of the plainer style of buildings, in which there is but little architectural detail to support parti-color treatment, no portion of the structure should be rendered glaringly prominent by the use of color. This would tend to give a loud or harsh appearance to the edifice, when really the opposite is what is sought. On the other hand, the contrast of color may be too tame, and then the general appearance will be dull and sombre. This is a frequent fault where the new colors are injudiciously used, where a rush is made from the hard, harsh outlines of white or light shades for walls, and green or dark shades for blinds and trim, to the parti-color effects modern decoration is intended to produce. Many colors are entirely unsuited for exterior decoration, notably the primary colors in their lighter shades, even if used as complementaries to darker tints. Bright blue, orange, purple or green could not be employed for exterior decorative purposes without startling results, but red and green-blue in their deep shades, being respectively warm and cold, are both agreeably harmonious and a perfect contrast, as are also deep purple and green. The most widely different colors do not by any means make the best contrast, any more than will those bearing the closest resemblance to each other produce the best harmony. As a general rule, the lower we descend in the chromatic scale, the nearer we approach the deepest shades of the colors we use, the greater will be the variety of colors we shall safely be enabled to select from. Light colors require handling with the greatest care if lifeless harshness, a hard outline and chilling effect are to be avoided, while all contrast of very light with very dark colors, with either predominating in quantity, are equally objectionable. This rule also applies to colors that suggest light; yellow, for instance, with its various graduations through orange to red, and the light shades of violet and gray; the deeper reds, ranging from vermilion down, are suggestive of warmth, not light, and may be used judiciously with excellent effect. Choose such colors for your building as will not harshly contrast with each other so as to isolate any part to which they are applied, but at the same time those that will sufficiently differ to give life and warmth to the structure without rendering it disagreeably obtrusive. These effects can be more safely and readily produced with dark than with light colors, and this affords one good reason for their preference, except in special cases, to which we shall refer later, in modern exterior decoration.

CHOICE OF COLORS WITH REGARD TO SURROUNDINGS AND LOCATION.

Many of the suggestions concerning the choice of colors as regards their combination and contrast will apply equally well in the choice of colors according to the location of the structure on which they are to be employed, and its surroundings. What we wish to avoid, as in our selection of colors with regard to their fitness of association in the building, is anything that will render the effect of the painter's work in contrast with the surroundings, either harshly prominent or lifelessly dull, and this is a general rule that will apply to every structure, whether plain or of elaborate form. Ordinarily, as we before remarked, the dark, warm colors, dulled to prevent obtrusiveness in tint and glaring effect, on account alike of their restful subdued appearance, and the readiness with which they may be made to harmonize with their surroundings, are to be preferred, and especially where, on account of the construction or location of a building, it is desired to give it an air of stability of warmth and comfort. A house occupying an elevated site, for instance, particularly if seen from below, with the cold-tinted sky for a background, would always lack solidity in appearance, and even if sheltered by trees, would have a cheerless look when they lost their leaves, if painted in light colors. It should be remembered, too, that such a house would appear to recede from the vision according to the rule that makes dark or warm-colored objects look nearer, such as are light or cold colored more remote or smaller. A change to an agreeable combination of dark colors, relieved with a little warmth and brightness, would give a house so situated a more important air, a more substantial and far more comfortable aspect, and in place of being a distant and obtrusive white point in the landscape, the warmth and taste displayed in the coloring would bring it into increased and agreeable prominence. Even the plainest and most unpretentious dwelling so located, by judicious treatment could be rendered attractive.

A building near water, or on a sandy beach, for instance, where, while brightness is not lacking, color is scarce, admits of different treatment. Here the same modified colors should be employed, but they admit of the introduction of more pronounced effects; lighter shades may be used to advantage, though anything like glaring brightness must be carefully avoided. Especially where the building is intended for summer use, as in the case of a hotel, a lighter appearance should be produced. The deep shade of blue-green with red, which we quoted as an example of warm, rich decoration, may here, for instance, give place to browns and ochres, with a little Indian red, all dulled to secure softness in tone, and worked from the darker shades in the lower stories to a lighter prevailing tone above. Thus while a warm, substantial effect would also in this case be secured, the heavy contrast of the dark colors with the light sameness of the surroundings would be avoided. There are cases, however, in which the effects produced by an attractive deep green shade are very cool and agreeable.

A building surrounded with or backed by heavy foliage, and placed where the brightest light would only reach it to a limited extent, might have a dull and sombre appearance if painted in dark colors exclusively; and there are cases in which even the conventional white or the indefinite grays, drabs and yellowish brown shades are admissible, but they are not many, and the employment of such tints, in view of their cheerless appearance as soon as foliage disappears, should be as far as possible avoided.

Even the location of a building with regard to the light should be considered in the selection of the colors and decorative effect, the north light being whitish or bluish, the south light yellow and purple morning and evening, with excessive brightness at noon, the east and west having the yellow and purple of the rising and setting sun and the usual brightness of the day. Colors that the reflection of the bright strong lights changes in appearance, as, for instance, green, which acquires a yellower brighter cast; red, which is rendered more vivid in the bright sunlight and darker by twilight; gray, which by contrast with its surroundings appears deeper and warmer if dark, and inclined to assume a purplish hue and colder appearance if light; and blue, which at twilight appears much lighter than it really is, should be used with a due regard to these effects.

In selecting colors with regard to the appearance of neighboring buildings, as becomes necessary in town or village painting, or even where groups of houses are located in close proximity, too much care cannot be exercised. Here the difference between harmony by contrast and harmony by resemblance, to which we have heretofore referred, assumes special significance. Originality under such circumstances, a departure from the beaten track, is apt to be regarded with disfavor by those of conventional tendencies, but, at the same time, where combined with fitness as to place, circumstances and uses, it is one of the most important factors in artistic progress. It does not necessarily follow because white or the lightest tints for body, and green or darker shades of the body color for trimmings have been used exclusively for many years past for house decoration, regardless of the effect, that no innovation should be made. Such a sameness reveals not only lack of taste, but a paucity of ideas. At the same time, the old pattern houses especially, by which we mean those in which the characteristics of modern ornamental architecture do not appear, are somewhat difficult to treat effectively, and the production of some unique and attractive form of decoration is almost certain to find imitators until another phase of the old sameness and tasteless uniformity is the result. A certain method of using a combination of colors may be effective, but its effect is immediately deteriorated by the duplication of the design, particularly where this is undertaken without any regard to whether or not it is appropriate to any other structure than that on which it was originally employed, or whether it would suit other surroundings. By working out a harmonious contrast between the building we are decorating and those in its vicinity, we can really render them valuable auxiliaries to the effects we are seeking to produce. At the same time, our remarks as to the effects of light and distance on the appearance of different colors should not be forgotten, especially where we may desire to make a building appear near to or more remote from the observer.

SELECTION AND APPLICATION OF COLORS AS INFLUENCED BY THE SIZE AND STYLE OF A BUILDING.

Herein we have one of the most important factors in exterior decoration and house painting, and one that has until recently been entirely ignored. The light shades and white used indiscriminately on buildings of all sizes, are really only fit for the smallest houses, and are admissible then only under special circumstances. A large structure in white, with only the abrupt green relief, is a distressing object in any landscape, but one that was universal until the revival in artistic ideas took place. We have already dwelt at length on the advantages the present fashionable styles of architecture possess from the decorative point of view, and having also considered the contrasts and combination of colors, we can dismiss this branch of our subject in a few words. Our warnings against violent contrasts will suffice to show the error, unless there is good reason for a sharp distinction, in giving the mouldings, beams, etc., in a building undue prominence in the broad color spaces. However much they differ, it should be a harmonious difference under all circumstances. Even the frame of the building, where it shows, should not be treated as far as light and shade is concerned, in such a manner as to make it appear separate from the remainder of the structure, but only so as to suggest its solidity by the employment of darker colors. The unity of the building as a piece of construction should be carefully preserved, no matter how tempting may be the opportunities in the shape of diversified materials, quaint design, etc., for the protection of original particolor effects.

In this branch of our subject we encounter one of our most serious difficulties in the treatment of the plain style of house that still predominates to so large an extent throughout the country. It is rational enough to make a consistent contrast between the trim and the prominent parts in the building and the flat surfaces, but it is an unmistakable error in style and taste to attempt, by the use of two colors on the plain surface, to break it up. In place of the parti-color effects desired, we produce a piece of patch-work that will always proclaim its incongruity, and the greater the contrast the worse it will cause the building to appear. Even the introduction of an artificial cornice or moulding does not suffice to disguise the violence done to the artistic appearance of the structure. In decorating the exterior of a building of the ordinary flat, square form, the more quiet tints and contrasts should prevail, and the brighter colors, introduced to afford relief and heighten the effect, should be used as sparingly as possible. Such suggestions as we have made as to the effects of distance, light and surroundings, should be most carefully considered in painting this class of houses, anything that would tend to draw them forcibly into prominence should be studiously avoided, light colors or bright shades of color should on no account be used, and even the dark tints employed should be carefully dulled, the object being to secure a warm, cheerful, subdued effect.

Large plain buildings may be darker than those of smaller size, while an isolated structure will usually bear greater warmth and depth of coloring than one standing in a group or street. Finally, we would urge on our readers the necessity for avoiding the idea, that what will look well on one structure will look equally well on another. The proportions, the form, the location of a building, may render the decoration found so attractive on another structure positively objectionable, and no style should be accepted on account of its beauty and fitness in one class of building without due consideration as to its adaptability to another. Imitation may be sincere, but it is often a very disastrous form of admiration in decorative art.

The uses to which a building are to be put should also exercise some influence on the choice of colors; a hotel, for instance, sometimes admits of brighter treatment than a private dwelling without any serious offense against good taste, especially if located near a lake or on the beach. In a building devoted to ecclesiastical purposes, the employment of a great variety of colors does not show a due regard for the fitness of things, though warm rich coloring is by no means out of place in such structures. The olives, the sage and dark blue-greens, with red relief, may give place to well-harmonized quiet shades of brown, a little lighter than would perhaps be selected for residence purposes, or gray tints may be preferred, the effect being wrought out in harmony of resemblance rather than in harmony by contrast. The season during which the structure will be used, where it is not intended for constant occupation, should also be allowed to exercise some influence. A building that is only open during the summer months may with advantage be decorated in lighter colors than one intended for winter occupation, but it is best in case of a residence to err, if any doubt is entertained, on the side of deep warm tints.

A few words on the decoration of extraordinary structures will enable us to conclude this chapter. The decorative treatment of such works as iron bridges, elevated railroads, etc., has already begun to attract the attention of the community. It is not by any means necessary that they should render our streets as hideous as they do. Though it would, perhaps, be impossible to make them altogether attractive in appearance, yet, by softening their outlines and employing colors that would not prove obtrusively harsh and disagreeably prominent, they might certainly be rendered less objectionable, and without detracting from their durability or employing pigments deficient in protective value. Iron bridges might in the same manner, especially in country places, be rendered unobjectionable if not attractive features in a landscape, by decorative treatment in conformance with the ideas and suggestions to which we have given expression. We might sum up these remarks in the following few words of advice to painters and those using paints: Avoid in decoration all such attempts at forced display or prominence in style or coloring as are obtained by the employment of harsh contrasts in color or arrangement of light and shade. Let good taste rather than bright attractiveness render your work conspicuous; above all, recollect that simplicity, in which is included perfect harmony in color and design, is the acme of art in decoration. The more natural we can make our buildings appear in associating their decorative effects with their surroundings, the more successful we are in imparting the idea that in their fitness and attractiveness they are part and parcel of the location, the nearer we come to the truest form of artistic decoration.

With the above remarks we conclude the artistic portion of our subject, and having thus fully referred to the selection of colors with regard to their intrinsic effects, their surroundings, and the nature and uses of the structures on which they are to be employed, we can proceed to discuss briefly and from a more practical standpoint, the paints themselves.

A CHAPTER ON PAINTS.

So far, the decorative value of paints and pigments, their selection with regard to effect alone, has come under our consideration, but we must not lose sight of the utility of the painter's art, which demands that these paints shall possess a certain durability and protective power. We have shown how in early art the decorative value only of a paint was considered, and it would almost seem as though the tendency in modern times is more or less in a similar direction. The widespread introduction of the modern ornamental colors, the dark greens, olives, maroons, etc., in which the leads and other materials hitherto relied on to give body and durability to the paint (although, as we shall proceed to show, the supposition was erroneous), could not be used with good effect, opened the door for the introduction of combinations of ingredients bearing the name of paints, and possessing a temporary decorative value, that were entirely worthless as far as any protective effect was concerned.

In order to be able to select a paint as to quality, and to form some approximate idea of its value and purity, a knowledge of the nature of a good paint and of the work it is intended to perform is necessary.

Paints are applied to the exterior of buildings, apart from the desire for the production of an ornamental effect, on account of their waterproofing properties. If of good quality, they form a coating on the surface of the wood or other substance that moisture cannot penetrate. A good paint, therefore, forms an impenetrable covering in the first place, its body is sufficient to obviate porosity and to cause the perfect cohesion of its particles, while at the same time it is of such a character as to ensure the economical distribution of the paint over the surface to which it is to be applied. In addition to this the paint must possess a certain amount of hardness, to enable it to withstand the friction of the rain and wind, and of the dust particles carried violently against its surface; sufficient toughness to enable it to resist ordinary abrasion or friction without sustaining injury, and sufficient elasticity to enable it to remain uninjured by the contraction and expansion of the surface to which it is applied incidental to changes of temperature. These qualifications no paint can possess unless the liquid ingredients are in proper chemical combination with the solid elements.

A fact chemists were prompt to recognize, and one of the features on which the popularity of the different leads and zincs have been based, was that they all formed a sort of saponaceous union with certain elements in the oil. Paints in which the liquids merely hold the solids in suspension or mechanical mixture, can never possess durability, their liquids are absorbed by the wood, or chemically changed by the atmosphere or evaporation into solids, leaving solid components on the surface in dry form to be scattered by the first breeze, or washed off by the first rain. Barytes does not unite with paint oil at all, and yet it is one of the commonest ingredients in the cheap preparations that have brought such discredit on the name of ready mixed paints. We must have in a good paint, substances that form a perfect combination, that cannot, even when applied as a coating to any surface, be separated or divided, and the ingredients must at the same time aid in hardening the oil. This white lead does not do; on the contrary, the acids employed and generated in its production are inherent factors in its destruction, and therefore we have so many complaints—especially where painters have been deceived as to the quality of the lead supplied them—concerning the quality of their paints, as well as a strong point against the exclusive use of white or light shades produced with the aid of white lead in exterior decoration, from an economical point of view.

Owing, in large part, to the growing extent to which buyers of paint were recognizing these facts, and to the increasing demand for the dark modern shades, in which the old zincs and whites could not be used as a paint body, as well as to their conviction that the time had come when really excellent ready mixed paints ought to secure recognition, the firm of F. W. Devoe & Co., one of the oldest and most extensive and successful paint manufacturing houses in the trade, turned their attention to the production of a superior line of house paints in ready mixed form. Not content with basing their claims to the patronage of painters and others on the prestige of their high reputation for honesty in their materials, which they manufacture from the initial processes and can consequently guarantee, and the skill, combined with the best of appliances, of which they avail themselves in their manipulation, they earnestly studied the subject both as practical painters and paint makers and chemists. They introduced valuable improvements in the preparation of the oil, with a view to increasing its hardening and elastic properties, they perfected the processes for manufacturing the different dry colors, and succeeded in producing new combinations of pigments, whereby a "body" was secured free from the objections to which the lead and zinc and crudely handled oil were open, and experience and practical use for a number of years has shown that their productions possess all the advantages required in a perfect paint, both in economy, in covering properties and facility of application, and in durability.

When the subject comes to be fairly considered, there is plainly every reason why colors supplied ready mixed by so well known a concern should be superior to any produced by hand. The painter buying his material in small quantities, however honest his intentions and however carefully he may work, labors under many disadvantages. He cannot always rely on the quality of his colors, his pigments, his oils, etc., he must mix his paints by hand and in small quantities, and cannot hope to secure the proper thoroughness in incorporation. He cannot always command the same make of colors and ingredients, and if his formulæ are never so carefully followed, the materials one concern supplies will nine times out of ten produce results different from those furnished by another. Then again, with the materials at his command and of which he has the knowledge, he cannot produce the colors and results modern decoration demands.

By the use of ready mixed paints, on the other hand, provided he is careful to procure them from a responsible concern, he is enabled not only to accomplish more work, but far better results within a given time, than was possible where he had to perform personally the entire work of mixing his colors.

Ready mixed paints supplied by such a firm as F. W. Devoe & Co., who themselves produce the dry colors from their first origin and all materials used in their manufacture, who have made their preparation with a view to their employment for exterior decorative purposes a specialty, who have facilities for the perfect mixing and grinding of the materials in such quantities as to ensure uniformity, and who have a reputation that is in itself a valuable protection to patrons, must naturally be superior to any that can be produced by hand, and by using them, the painter is freed from the trouble, risk and *responsibility* that attaches to the mixing and preparation of paints. Not only this, but he is able to select his colors from an immense assortment, in place of having to produce the tints he requires one after another, without having an opportunity to judge of their appearance alone or in combination; he is spared the trouble and difficulty of groping after effects in decoration which, with the colors before him, he is able to determine on without hesitation. Ready mixed paints are, moreover, an advantage to the painter in modern times, with the competition and striving after the highest excellence that is evident in every craft, and who, if he is desirous of maintaining a position in the front rank among his fellow-tradesmen, should have long since developed from a mere color-mixer into an artist.

It cannot be denied that considerable prejudice exists in reference to the employment of ready mixed paints. The trade has been injured so seriously by the operations of unscrupulous manufacturers, who have placed the worst possible trash on the market in the guise of ready mixed paints, that not only painters, but all for whom paints are used, look upon their purchase in this form with considerable doubt. Where they are supplied by an old established house, with a high reputation for the possession of honest intentions towards their customers, and the ability, facilities and resources that enable them to put these intentions into practice, this feeling should not operate against an article the value of which experience has fully demonstrated, while painters, for reasons we have already given, should regard the wholesale manufacturer of first-class ready mixed paints as a friend and assistant in their business, instead of in the light of a competitor.

PRACTICAL SUGGESTIONS TO THE PAINTER.

If the painter, or the person using paints, will bear in mind what we have previously stated with regard to the properties of a perfect paint, many things will suggest themselves to him as absolutely necessary to avoid in order to ensure successful work.

Good paint covers the surface to which it is applied with a waterproof film. The more perfect and durable its impermeability, the better the paint. It is designed to protect the surface to which it is applied against the destructive effects of moisture—the most active element in promoting decay—and should, therefore, only be applied to a thoroughly dry surface or substance, *for it will keep moisture in as well as out*. The decay of sappy wood, due to the effect of the fermenting vegetable moisture, is naturally heightened by coating the wood with a substance that keeps such moisture in the wood against all hope of evaporation, and the same may be advanced with regard to such moisture as the wood absorbs. Care should be taken, therefore, to apply a paint *only on a dry surface*, (and substance) otherwise it will inevitably blister, owing to the issue of moisture from the pores beneath it in the shape of vapor; the gases of decay may also puff up the paint skin, if it is good paint and strong enough to withstand the distention; it may also crack and peel off from the same cause, or lose its gloss, turn blotchy or dull. Even if applied when there is dampness in the atmosphere, although the surface on which it is used may apparently be perfectly dry, a similar effect may be produced, and carelessness in applying paint on damp days or to a damp surface is a frequent cause of trouble, bringing discredit on the painter, the manufacturer of the paint, and the article itself. Not only this, but the presence of moisture prepares the substance of the wood for the attack of the dry rot organism, which at first softens the wood, causing paint to lose its hold and peel off, and finally effects the total destruction of the wood substance.

What we have suggested concerning the application of paints will apply with equal force to the employment of priming coats, which are used in the first place to protect the upper stratum of the fibre substance of the wood against the attacks of moisture from either direction, to preserve it so that the paint may remain firmly attached to it. It can readily be seen that if the surface be impregnated with moisture, the spaces the priming is designed to enter will be more or less occupied by watery particles, and it cannot therefore penetrate to do its work. The priming, in the second place, is designed to prepare the surface for the paint and prevent the too rapid absorption of the latter. It should consequently be as thin as possible to secure its penetration, of such a nature as to ensure its drying near the surface instead of being too rapidly absorbed or (as in cases where turpentine or benzine is used in primers) evaporated. Finally, it should be of such a character as to unite readily with the oil in the paint, if we do not wish the latter to peel off, and therefore in most successful dryers we find a very large proportion of oil. Some painters use oil alone, under certain conditions, with the most satisfactory results.

It is needless to admonish painters of the necessity for allowing the priming to dry thoroughly before paint is applied to its surface, and the same remarks must apply to the conditions to be observed in putting on the second coat, etc. If the weather has been unfavorable to the drying of one of the coats, a favorable change in the atmosphere should be awaited; under no circumstances should one coat go over another while it is not perfectly dry, or while any sign of dampness or moisture appears on its surface. To the finishing coat these remarks apply with special force, and if not observed the result will be spotting, dullness and lack of durability.

The priming should be flowed evenly over the entire surface and well rubbed in; the first coat of paint should be worked in with extra thoroughness, filling all pores, cracks, etc., and forming a good foundation for subsequent coats, which should be applied with the even finish that is acquired only by a practised use of the brush. Before priming, in new work, knots and "fat" places in wood, which by their resinous exudations spoil all colors and often cause cracking, chipping, etc., should be thoroughly killed, an application of shellac varnish being the best medium for this purpose; in the case of a troublesome knot, a hot iron may be used to draw out the rosin, or if very bad, the spot should be cut out cleanly and the hole properly stopped. After the first coat of paint is dry, every crack or aperture should be carefully puttied and a smooth surface prepared for the finishing coat. Some painters prefer a dark, others a light color for their priming, leaving the finishing coat to be the lightest of all; this is, however, a matter of technical taste, though it is usually considered advisable to have a dark background to work on.

The ready mixed paints sent out by F. W. Devoe & Co., are, as their name implies, *ready for use*, and contain all that is necessary in a first class paint. In cold weather, which has a tendency to thicken all paints, the least possible addition of spirits of turpentine may be allowed as thinning, but it should be used only in barely sufficient quantity to effect the desired result; at other times where a thin coat is desired, a small quantity of raw linseed oil may be used; any addition of benzine or other common adulterant will impair at once the appearance and the durability of the paint.

With these instructions and suggestions as to the selection and use of colors, which we respectfully dedicate to the public in general and our painters in particular, either the painter or the property owner should be enabled, with the exercise of due intelligence, to accomplish the tasteful and effective exterior decoration as well as the protection and preservation of a building, in such a manner as to increase its durability, and at the same time render it an agreeable object to contemplate from a distance or near by ; a harmonious feature amidst the plainest or the most picturesque surroundings.

With a view to the practical demonstration of the correctness of the principles we have enunciated in the foregoing chapters, and as a means of illustrating the effects that can be produced by a judicious and artistic use of colors, we present in the following pages, a series of Plates showing some methods of decorative treatment applied to buildings of diversified styles and with varied surroundings.

Our object has been in these Plates to illustrate an average selection of *existing* buildings, both modern and old-fashioned, in order to ensure the universal utility of the work; at the same time we regard our Plates only as suggestions, upon which the painter can enlarge at pleasure to such an extent as the colors at his command will allow, without, however, losing sight of artistic and tasteful effect.

In our Plates every condition as to the location, form, exterior design, etc., of the buildings represented has been carefully studied, and we reproduce the actual appearance, taking light and shade and other important factors into consideration, that such structures would present if treated with the colors enumerated, and in the manner described in the notes accompanying each illustration.

NOTE —The numbers in the descriptive matter accompanying each Plate refer to the tabulated Color Charts to be found on pages 94, 95, at the end.

PLATE I represents a private residence in the vicinity of New York, built in the modern " Queen Anne" style of architecture. The building occupying an elevated site, stands near the highway and in a somewhat exposed situation, there being but little foliage or variation of color in the surroundings.

The effect desired was richness and warmth of appearance and the avoidance of all violent contrasts in the building itself and with the landscape.

To accomplish this the following combination of colors was employed :

Body, First Story, - - - - - - -	No. 662
" Second Story, - - - - - - -	" 608
Trimming, - - - - - - - -	" 588
Blinds, - - - - - - - - -	" 652
Sashes, - - - - - - - - -	" Black.
Peaks and Sides of Dormer, - - - - - -	" 651

The roof, of shingles, was left in the condition caused by exposure to the elements, but the same color could be produced in new shingle work by the employment of a stain made with copperas solution.

Plate I

PLATE II shows the same building depicted in the previous plate treated with a view to bringing it into greater prominence by the production of a bolder, brighter effect.

It will be observed that the general appearance of the house is still warmer and better adapted, for instance, to a winter landscape or surroundings in which cold or neutral tints prevail, than the previous design.

The combination of colors used is:

Body, First Story, - - - - - - -	No. 580
" Second Story, - - - - - - -	" 658
Trimming, - - - - - - - -	" 652
Blinds, - - - - - - - -	" 651
Sashes, - - - - - - - - -	" 582
Peaks and Sides of Dormers, - - - - -	" 662
Roof, - - - - - - - - -	" 651

Plate II

Forbes Co.Boston & N.Y.

PLATE III represents a style of building first erected in the Eastern and Middle States about twenty-five years ago and still very popular. The original design was taken from an Italian villa residence, and houses of this type, on account of their spacious interiors and reasonable cost of construction, are still built in all parts of the country.

Our combination of colors, adapted to almost any surroundings, represents the first transition from the original white and delicate neutral tints, and is intended to produce a somewhat more substantial effect than the former were capable of, preserving, however, their cool appearance in a subdued form.

We use the following colors:

Body,	No. 541
Trimming,	" 534
Blinds,	" 581
Sashes,	" 587

Plate III

PLATE IV. Here we illustrate the same building represented in Plate III, a brighter and more prominent effect being desired.

The house in this case may be supposed to stand in near proximity to other structures, and the design is therefore adapted for village or town purposes as well as for isolated buildings.

The body color in the front of the house is intensified by the strong sunlight falling on it; the actual tint is best shown in the shadows.

The colors used are:

Body,	No. 526
Trimming,	" 608
Blinds,	" 651
Sashes,	" 608

Plate IV

Forbes Co Boston & N.Y.

PLATE V shows the same building as the two preceding plates illustrate, but the combination of colors is intended to give it a richer, warmer appearance.

A house so colored would form, under similar conditions, a helpful and agreeable contrast to either of the two previous styles of decoration adopted for the building.

The colors comprise :

Body,	No. 656
Trimming,	" 654
Blinds,	" 651
Sashes,	" 608

Plate V

PLATE VI. The residence of a prominent South American Government official, built in the United States and erected in the Argentine Republic.

Being in a hot climate, with tropical surroundings as to foliage, etc., a cool effect was necessary and neutral tints only, relieved with brighter colors, were selected, the ornate design of the building itself greatly facilitating their employment.

The colors used are:

Body, - - - - - - - - -	No. 591
Trimming and Sash, - - - - - - -	" 534
Blinds, - - - - - - - - -	" 544

The roof is of slate of a natural bluish shade.

In PLATE VII the building depicted in Plate VI is again represented, but a brighter and more conspicuous appearance has been produced by the use of livelier colors.

At the same time it will be observed that any tendency towards warmth or heaviness has been carefully and successfully avoided.

Body, - - - - - - - - - No. 595
Trimming, - - - - - - - - - " 527
Blinds, - - - - - - - - - " 651
Sashes, - - - - - - - - Color Same as Body.

Plate VII

Forbes Co. Boston & N.Y.

PLATE VIII. The style of house here represented is very prevalent and deservedly popular in all parts of the country. It is economical as far as cost of construction is concerned, spacious and commodious, and when treated with due regard to taste in decoration is capable of making an excellent appearance.

Where the house occupies a prominent position, the coloring shown will be found effective and appropriate. The contrast between the window shades in the upper and lower stories, and the general effect is worth noting.

Body,	-	-	-	-	-	-	-	-	No. 651
Trimming,	-	-	-	-	-	-	-	-	" 654
Blinds,	-	-	-	-	-	-	-	-	" 589
Sashes,	-	-	-	-	-	-	-	-	" 539 or Black.
Roof,	-	-	-	-	-	-	-	-	" 588

Plate VIII

In PLATE IX the same house is shown that has been illustrated in Plate VIII, the location being similar, and a quieter but yet a warm effect being sought.

The colors used are:

Body,	No. 661
Trimming,	" 663
Blinds,	" 652
Sashes,	" 651
Roof,	" 587

Plate IX

Forbes Co. Boston & N.Y.

In PLATE X the building shown in the two previous illustrations is supposed to be located in an isolated position, in a hilly country or remote from the highway or point of observation.

The bright, bold effect is peculiarly suited for such conditions, or where a building is surrounded by heavy foliage, but would not constitute an agreeable contrast with other buildings that might be located in the vicinity.

The local surroundings in our plate are the same as previously shown:

Body, - - - - - - - - - No. 580
Trimming, - - - - - - - - - " 653
Blinds, - - - - - - - - - " 589
Sashes, - - - - - - - - - " 583
Roof, - - - - - - - - California Redwood Shingles

Plate X

PLATE XI.   The tendency of modern transportation companies to render their various structures as attractive as possible, and the consequent increase in the demand for technical skill in the accomplishment of this object, induces us to present an illustration of a depot on the Pennsylvania Railroad, the coloring of which is intended to produce a bright and striking effect.

The surroundings are somewhat open, as is usual with buildings of this nature, but it will be noticed that the depot is skilfully set off by the well kept grounds.

The colors used are:

Body, First Story,   -   -   -   -   -   -   -   No. 650

   "   Second Story,   -   -   -   -   -   -   -   " 654

Trimming,   -   -   -   -   -   -   -   -   " 653

Sashes,   -   -   -   -   -   -   -   -   " 525

The roof is a combination of blue and green slate.

Plate XI

EMMETT STREET

Forbes Co. Boston & N.Y.

PLATE XII. The production of a rich and elegant effect being desired in the depot described in Plate XI, a combination of deeper, warmer tints has been employed with a most pleasing result.

We have used:

Body, First Story,	No. 651
" Second Story,	" 654
Trimming,	" 652
Sashes,	" 525

Plate XII

EMMETT STREET

Forbes Co. Boston & N.Y.

PLATE XIII.   The old style country dwelling, typical in its lack of all architectural ornamentation of the plain tastes and habits of the early settlers in the New England States, and of which many are still to be found, is here depicted treated in conventional style—painted plain white with green blinds.

The cold, glaring effect is always harsh amid any surroundings, but the form of the house has been regarded as almost prohibitory of any attempt at artistic treatment.

In Plate XIV we offer a suggestion as to what might be accomplished with a house of this style.

Plate XIII

PLATE XIV. At an expense of about twenty-five or thirty dollars belt courses of four-inch tongue and groove boarding have been substituted for sections of the clap-boarding of our old-fashioned house, effectually breaking up the flat side-wall surfaces, allowing of a contrast in color and effect between the first and second stories, and architecturally changing the entire appearance of the structure.

The style of decoration would be adapted to almost any locality.

Body, First Story, - - - - - - - No. 611
" Second Story, - - - - - - - " 589
Belt Courses and Trimming, - - - - - " 656
Blinds, - - - - - - - - - " 652
Sashes, - - - - - - - - - " 651

The roof of shingles is left the natural weather-beaten color.

Plate XIV

PLATE XV.   In order to show the importance of care in the selection of colors in the production of the harmony in contrast to which we have referred in our chapter on the " Artistic Selection and Combination of Colors," we illustrate two houses, differing in design, but represented in close proximity to each other and under similar conditions as to surrondings.

The general effect is rich, warm and elegant, the architectural details being brought into agreeable prominence.   The colors used in the house on the right hand side of the picture are:

Body, - - - - - - - - -	No. 605
Trimming, - - - - - - - - -	" 652
Blinds, - - - - - - - -	" 651
Sashes, - - - - - - - - -	" 655
Peaks and Gable Fronts, - - - - - -	" 650
Roof, - - - - - - - - - -	" 587

In the house to the left of the picture we have used:

Body, - - - - - - - - -	No. 650
Trimming, - - - - - - - - -	" 611
Blinds, - - - - - - - - -	" 652
Peaks, Shingle Work, Sashes and Belts around House, -	" 605
Roof, - - - - - - - - -	" 589

Plate XV

PLATE XVI shows the same houses illustrated in the preceding number, a different plan of decorative treatment having been adopted.

The general effect is a little more subdued, but equal prominence has been given to the picturesque architectural features of both buildings.

In the right hand house we use:

Body, Peaks, and Gable Fronts, - - - - -	No. 589
Trimming, - - - - - - - -	" 651
Blinds, - - - - - - - -	" 652
Roof, - - - - -	Natural Weather Beaten Shingles.

For the decoration of the house on the left of our picture there has been employed:

Body, - - - - - - - -	No. 651
Trimming, - - - - - - - -	" 589
Blinds, - - - - - - - -	" 609
Roof, Shingle Work and Belts around House, - - -	" 589

Plate XVI

PLATE XVII.   We have endeavored in this illustration to give some idea of the decoration of a building located on a lofty elevation and seen only from a distance, as is the case with many hotels and summer places of residence throughout the country.   The object is to produce a bold, striking appearance, in contrast with the landscape and forming in it, from a remote point of observation, a prominent but agreeable feature.

This can only be accomplished by a tasteful and judicious employment of the brightest and most brilliant colors, even the chrome yellow shown in our plate producing an agreeable effect.

We have used:

Body,	No. 585
Trimming and Blinds,	" 651
Sashes,	" 589

The roof is slate, *of a natural* bluish color.

In PLATE XVIII we have the hotel building shown in Plate XVII, treated with a view to the production of a richer and more substantial appearance, the harmony with the surrounding landscape being more subdued, but equally agreeable, and the building from the customary points of observation still prominent.

The colors used are:

Body,	No. 651
Trimming,	" 536
Blinds,	" 589
Sashes,	" 652

Plate XVII Plate XVIII

Forbes Co. Boston & N.Y.

PLATE XIX.   The residence here shown, of excellent proportions and erected in an attractive style of architecture, is located in Connecticut and situated at such an elevation and with such open surroundings as to have from almost all points of view, the sky as a background.

Painted in light neutral shades it presented a cold, unsubstantial appearance, and in order to give it an air of warmth and solidity, and at the same time a certain cheerful prominence, the colors shown in our design were suggested.

They are :

Body, - - - - - - - -	No. 589
Trimming, - - - - - - - -	" 651
Blinds, - - - - - - - -	" 652
Sashes, - - - - - - - -	" 587

Roof, slate of natural blue aud green tints.

Plate XIX

In PLATE XX a second suggestion for the decoration of the building shown in Plate XIX is illustrated, which as developing greater warmth and richness of effect, securing the desired solidity of appearance and at the same time producing a still more satisfactory contrast with the surroundings, was finally adopted, with entirely satisfactory results.

The colors employed were:

Body,	No. 651
Trimming,	" 652
Blinds,	" 588
Sashes,	" 582

Plate XX

Forbes Co Boston & N.Y.

The Harrison Bros. Color Card

COLOR NUMBER	NATIONAL BUREAU OF STANDARDS COLOR NAMES	MUNSELL NOTATION
1	Dark Green	7.5 G 3/4
3	Grayish Blue	5 PB 4/2
4	Grayish Blue	2.5 PB 5/4
5	Bluish Gray	10 B 6/1
6	Light Yellowish Green	2.5 G 7/4
7	Strong Yellowish Brown	7.5 YR 5/6
8	Dark Orange Yellow	8.5 YR 5.5/8
10	Dark Orange Yellow	7.5 YR 6/8
11	Moderate Orange Yellow	7.5 YR 7/6
12	Pale Orange Yellow	9 YR 7.5/4
13	Grayish Reddish Brown	10 R 3/2
15	Grayish Brown	7.5 YR 3/2
16	Grayish Brown	7.5 YR 4/2
17	Light Grayish Brown	7.5 YR 5/3
19	Moderate Olive Brown	2.5 Y 3/2
20	Grayish Olive	5 Y 4/2
21	Olive Gray	5 Y 4/1
22	Light Olive Brown	2.5 Y 4.5/2
23	Light Grayish Yellowish Brown	10 YR 6/2
25	Moderate Reddish Brown	7.5 R 3/6
28	Grayish Red	5 R 5/4
29	Moderate Yellowish Pink	7.5 R 7/4
31	Dark Grayish Reddish Brown	7.5 R 2/2
34	Grayish Red	7.5 R 5/2
35	Strong Reddish Brown	10 R 3/10
36	Deep Reddish Orange	7.5 R 4/12
37	Moderate Reddish Orange	1.5 YR 5/10
38	Dark Orange Yellow	7.5 YR 6.3/10
39	Brilliant Yellow	5 Y 8/10
40	Pale Greenish Yellow	10 Y 8.5/4
41	Yellowish White	5 Y 9/1
42	Deep Yellowish Green	10 GY 4/8
43	Yellowish Gray	10 Y 7.5/1
44	Yellowish White	2.5 Y 8.5/2
45	Yellowish Gray	8 YR 7/2
46	Yellowish Gray	2.5 Y 8/2
47	Grayish Yellow	3.5 Y 8/3
48	Pale Yellowish Pink	7.5 YR 8/2
49	Light Neutral Gray	N 8.0/
50	Light Bluish Green	5 BG 7.3/4
51	Grayish Reddish Brown	7.5 R 3.5/2
52	Pinkish Gray	10 R 7/1

The Harrison Bros. Color Card was matched with the Munsell Notation. The discoloration of the small chips was accounted for in matching as closely as possible these 42 colors to the Munsell System.

Frank Sagendorph Welsh, Historic Architectural Finishes Consultant
P.O. Box 214, Ardmore, Pa.   19003

HARRISON BROS. & CO'S

TOWN AND COUNTRY

105 SO. FRONT ST. PHILAD'A.

16 BURLING SLIP NEW YORK.

READY PREPARED PAINTS.

FOR HOMESTEAD, COTTAGE AND VILLA USE.

ENTERED according to Act of Congress, in the Year 1871, by HARRISON BROS. & CO, in the Office of the LIBRARIAN of Congress, at Washington, D.C.

No. 49. Sanded. Berea Stone. Similar to Franklin Stone.

No. 12. Sanded. Massillon Stone.

No. 46. Sanded. Ohio Sand Stone, or Cleveland Stone.

No. 37. No. 38. No. 39. No. 40. No. 41. No. 42.

No. 31. No. 51. No. 34. No. 52. No. 35. No. 36.

No. 25. No. 28. No. 29. No. 48. No. 49. No. 50.

No. 19. No. 20. No. 21. No. 22. No. 23. No. 47.

No. 13. No. 15. No. 16. No. 17. No. 45. No. 46.

No. 7. No. 8. No. 10. No. 11. No. 12. No. 44.

No. 1. No. 3. No. 4. No. 5. No. 43. No. 6.

No. 51. Sanded. Connecticut Brown Stone. Ne Plus Ultra of Brown Stones. Perfect Imitation.

No. 26. Sanded. Seneca Stone.

No. 53. Sanded. Nova Scotia. "Dorchester."

F. W. DEVOE & COMPANY,

(Established 1852.)

Offices: corner of Fulton and William Streets, New York City.

Manufacturers of Fine Varnishes.

VARNISHES

OF EVERY DESCRIPTION,

For Exterior Work,

INCLUDING

CAR FINISHING,

COACH and CAR RUBBING,

COACH FINISHING,

SHIP COATING,

Etc.

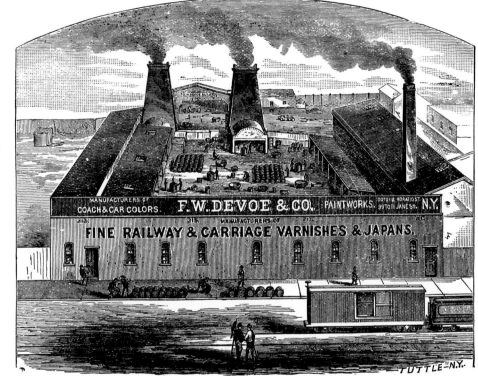

VARNISHES

OF EVERY DESCRIPTION,

For Interior Work,

INCLUDING

HARD OIL FINISH,

WOOD COATING,

WOOD FILLER,

COPAL, DAMAR,

Etc.

VARNISH WORKS: 213, 215, 217 and 219 RAILROAD AVENUE, NEWARK, NEW JERSEY.

Our Works for the manufacture of Varnishes, Japans, etc., are located in the city of Newark, New Jersey. They are very completely arranged and have every facility for the perfect production of the different classes of Varnish, such as Railway, Car, Fine Coach, Carriage, Copal, Damar, Black Japan and Liquid Dryers.

We have been engaged many years in the manufacture of the above, and have a large and valuable experience in that line.

Our goods have been long and favorably known, both at home and abroad, for their great superiority.

We shall continue to maintain their high standard of quality in the future as in the past, and our goods will be found to be fully equal in quality to those of European manufacture, and much lower in cost.

Our Fine Varnishes, after being exposed to severe competitive tests, have been adopted by many of the leading RAILWAY COMPANIES of the United States. Among them we may mention the Pennsylvania Railroad, New York Central Railroad, Manhattan Elevated Railroad, Brooklyn Elevated Railroad, Philadelphia & Reading Railroad, Pullman Palace Car Company, New York, Lake Erie & Western Railway, Long Island Railroad, and many others.

They will be found to be BRILLIANT and ELASTIC, and to possess all the important qualities of reliable Varnishes. They are put up in barrels, and in cans of every size, from one-half pint to five gallons each, labeled and carefully boxed for distant shipment; each package bearing our label and seal.

This department of our business is under the special direction of Mr. J. Seaver Page, of our firm.

SEND FOR SPECIAL CATALOGUE GIVING FULL INFORMATION.

F. W. DEVOE & COMPANY,

(Established 1852,)

Offices: corner Fulton and William Streets, New York City,

Manufacturers and Importers of Artists' Materials.

F. W. Devoe & Co's Canvas—in Rolls and on Stretchers

F. W. Devoe & Co's Japanned Tin Boxes for Oil Colors.

F. W. Devoe & Co's Artists' Oils, Varnishes, Mediums, &c.

F. W. Devoe & Co's Artists' Tube Colors.

F. W. Devoe & Co's Sketching Blocks, for Oil, Water Color and Pencil.

We publish a complete Illustrated Catalogue of 250 pages devoted entirely to the above goods.   In it will be found a descriptive Priced List of every requirement of an artist,

F. W. DEVOE & COMPANY,

(ESTABLISHED 1852.)

Offices: corner Fulton and William Streets, New York City.

Manufacturers of Fine Brushes

OF EVERY DESCRIPTION.

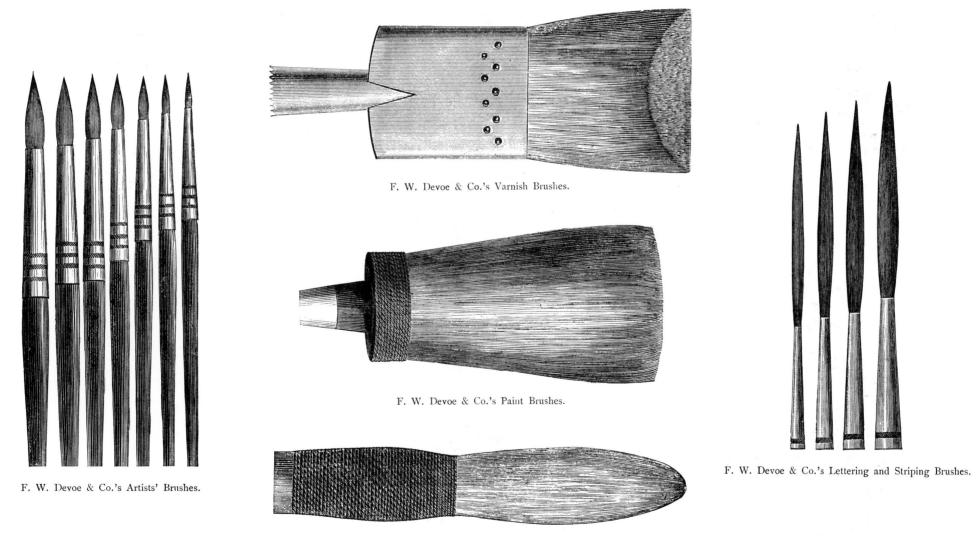

F. W. Devoe & Co.'s Varnish Brushes.

F. W. Devoe & Co.'s Paint Brushes.

F. W. Devoe & Co.'s Artists' Brushes.

F. W. Devoe & Co.'s Lettering and Striping Brushes.

F. W. Devoe & Co.'s Fresco Brushes.

We publish a complete Illustrated Catalogue of 88 pages of our Brush Department. We manufacture brushes of every description direct from the raw material, and the appointments of our Brush Factory are second to none in the country.

F. W. DEVOE & COMPANY,

(Established 1852,)

Offices: corner Fulton and William Streets, New York City,

Manufacturers of

THE HIGHEST GRADES OF READY MIXED PAINTS.

Attention is called to our sample pages, showing fifty of our more desirable shades.

The value of these Paints has been demonstrated by many years of practical use.

This is a fac-simile of our Label, which will be found on every package.

Our Ready Mixed Paints are made from the best materials only, and do not enter into competition with low-priced goods. Send for special Catalogue, showing samples of shades and giving full information.

F. W. DEVOE & COMPANY,

(Established 1852,)

Offices: Corner Fulton and William Streets, New York City.

Manufacturers of

THE HIGHEST GRADES OF READY MIXED PAINTS

FOR HOUSEHOLD USE.

IMPORTANT!

Please read this notice.

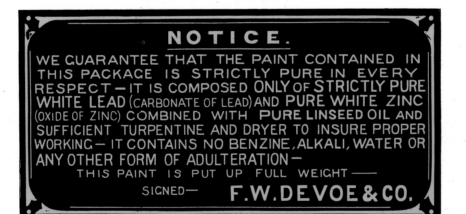

We put this guarantee on every package of Inside and Outside White, from a one pound can to a 40 gallon barrel.

Our Tints and Body Colors are composed of mineral colors and the most permanent pigments.

We use ONLY pure linseed oil in our Mixed Paints.

This is a fac-simile of our label which we put on small packages of Mixed Paint.

Sample Cards, containing 50 desirable tints and body colors, sent to any address on request.

F. W. DEVOE & COMPANY,

(ESTABLISHED 1852.)

Offices: corner Fulton and William Streets, New York City,

MANUFACTURERS OF

FLORENTINE FRESCO COLORS,

FOR FRESCO AND SCENE PAINTING.

LIST OF COLORS.

Antwerp Blue.
Blue Black.
Bremen Blue.
Brown Ochre.
Cobalt Blue.
Carmine Lake.
Carnation Lake.
Crimson Lake.
Chrome Green,—Light.
Chrome Green,—Medium.
Chrome Green,—Deep.
Cremnitz White.
Chrome Yellow,—Light.
Chrome Yellow,—Medium.
Chrome Yellow,—Deep.
Chrome Orange.

Dutch Pink.
Emerald Green.
English Vermilion,—Pale.
English Vermilion,—Deep
Florence Lake.
French Zinc White.
Gold Ochre.
Green Lake.
Ivory Black.
Indigo.
Italian Burnt Sienna.
Imperial Madder,—Light.
Imperial Madder,—Deep.
Italian Raw Sienna.
Italian Vandyke Brown.
Indian Red.

LIST OF COLORS.

Mountain Blue.
Maroon Lake.
Mauve Lake.
Magenta Lake.
Milori Yellow,—Light.
Milori Yellow,—Deep.
Milori Green,—Light.
Milori Green,—Medium.
Milori Green,—Deep.
Naples Yellow.
Olive Green,—Light.
Olive Green,—Medium.
Olive Green,—Deep,
Old Gold.
Prussian Blue.
Purple Lake.

Roman Ochre.
Roman Ochre,—Extra Deep.
Scarlet Lake.
Solferino Lake.
Sepia.
Turkey Burnt Umber.
Turkey Raw Umber.
Turkey Red,—Light.
Turkey Red,—Deep.
Ultramarine Blue.
Ultramarine Green,—Light.
Ultramarine Green,—Deep.
Ultramarine,--Violet.
Venetian Red.
Yellow Ochre.

These are carefully selected Superfine Colors, and prepared in a pulp state—without glue or sizing, for the use of Fresco and Scene Painters. They are very finely ground and will be found much more desirable than the usual Distemper Colors. These Colors are packed in round, clear white glass jars carefully covered and bladdered. The jars are of one size—about 3¾ inches high by 2⅝ inches in diameter (as per cut above).

SPECIAL LARGE PACKAGES FOR CONSUMERS. CATALOGUES CONTAINING SAMPLES OF ALL THE ABOVE COLORS SENT ON REQUEST.

We keep a full line of Fresco Designs, Brushes and other materials for decoration.

F. W. DEVOE & COMPANY,

(ESTABLISHED 1852.)

Offices: corner Fulton and William Streets, New York City,

MANUFACTURERS OF

FINEST GRADES OF COLORS,

GROUND IN PURE LINSEED OIL.

Fac-simile of our Label used on our BEST GRADE.

During the past few years many manufacturers have largely deteriorated the quality of their highest grades of Oil Colors by grinding them in *inferior oils*, such as "Rosin Oil," Petroleum Products, etc., instead of "*Pure Linseed Oil*," and also by using *inferior grades of pigments*. We have, on the contrary, not only resolutely maintained our high standard of absolute purity, but have made many improvements in our *shades*, etc., which have, as a consequence, given our colors the highest reputation among the best class of painters.

We claim that our colors, taking both their quality and price into consideration, are for the *consumer* the most economical ever manufactured.

We publish the most complete Color Catalogue, of 135 pages, ever issued, giving full description of our goods, fac-similes of our Labels, etc.

F. W. DEVOE & COMPANY,

(Established 1852.)

Offices: corner Fulton and William Streets, New York City,

MANUFACTURERS OF

FINEST GRADES OF DRY COLORS,

DIRECT FROM THE RAW MATERIAL.

CHROME YELLOWS.

CHROME GREENS.

PRUSSIAN BLUE.

CHINESE BLUE.

PARIS BLUE.

OCHRES.

UMBERS.

SIENNAS.

TRADE MARK.

VERMILIONS.

"ZUBIA" VERMILION,

(A Substitute for Quicksilver Vermilion.)

"PERSIAN SCARLET."

TUSCAN REDS.

INDIAN REDS.

IVORY BLACKS.

ORANGE MINERAL.

FINE LAKES.

We are large manufacturers of Dry Colors direct from the raw material, and also have an extensive correspondence with English, French and German Color Makers, and large storage facilities at our Works. We are, therefore, enabled to have constantly on hand a full stock of Dry Colors, such as are used by Paint Grinders, Decorators, Paper Stainers, Lithographers, Printing Ink Makers, Etc., Etc.

F. W. DEVOE & COMPANY,

(Established 1852.)

Offices: Corner Fulton and William Streets, New York City.

Specialties for Interior and Exterior Woodwork.

WAX FINISH.

For finishing interior woodwork where a soft, oily appearance is desired, and is designed to be used in place of varnish where hard or stained woods are used. It is also serviceable for coating wood floors.

ZANZORITE.

An elastic and durable Varnish for coating the exterior of buildings where a handsome finish is desired. Houses painted in dark shades which have become dull can have their lustre and color renewed by using Zanzorite.

WOOD STAINS.

For staining soft woods in perfect imitation of the natural hard woods. We make Rosewood, Mahogany, Cherry, Ebony, Black Walnut, Chestnut, and Light and Dark Oak Stains.

HARD OIL FINISH.

For finishing interior woodwork where a hard, glossy finish is desired. This is very durable, and has always given absolute satisfaction. We make "Light Oil Finish," for light woods, and "Hard Oil Finish," for dark woods.

PASTE WOOD FILLER.

For filling the grain of hard woods. It fills the pores of the wood thoroughly, giving a soft, smooth finish without grit, so that a brilliant surface is obtained with but one coat of varnish.

SHIP COATING.

A tough and elastic finish for all exposed parts of vessels, such as spars, masts, woodwork, cabins, etc. This is specially designed to withstand the action of the elements.

FRENCH ZINC.

Green and Red Seal, in Poppy Oil.

We grind strictly pure French Zinc in poppy oil for inside finishing where a pure white surface, which will not turn yellow, is desired.

GRAINING COLORS.

For graining woods in imitation of Light and Dark Oak, Chestnut, Walnut, Mahogany, etc. These colors are especially prepared so as to work to the best advantage under the graining tool. Will dry in twelve hours.

INSIDE WHITE LEAD.

We manufacture this lead specially for inside work. It has great covering properties, works remarkably smooth under the brush, and is particularly adapted for hotel work. Will not turn yellow.

WRITE FOR CIRCULARS GIVING FULL DESCRIPTION.

F. W. DEVOE & COMPANY,

(ESTABLISHED 1852.)

Offices: corner Fulton and William Streets, New York City,

MANUFACTURERS OF

COACH AND CAR COLORS,

GROUND IN JAPAN,

For the Special Use of Coach, Car and Carriage Painters.

Fac-simile of Label used on Can.

These Colors are made with great care, and ground from dry materials and Japans manufactured in our own Factories. We are thereby enabled to guarantee their perfect purity. They have been largely used for the past ten years in the leading Car and Carriage Shops of the United States.

We publish a Catalogue and Priced List, giving full information and to which is attached finished samples of Colors.

F. W. DEVOE & COMPANY,

(Established 1852.)

Offices: corner Fulton and William Streets, New York City,

MANUFACTURERS OF

ELASTIC ROOF COATING,

MIXED READY FOR USE.

In Two Shades—Brown and Red.

SPECIALLY ADAPTED FOR USE ON METALLIC ROOFS.

There is no surface to which paint is applied that receives such severe wear as the roofs of buildings, railway cars, etc., as they are constantly exposed to the action of the elements, and to keep them in good condition by the use of ordinary roofing paints it is necessary to re-coat them frequently.

Many of the roofing paints heretofore manufactured have been found, after short exposure, to CRACK BADLY or disappear in the form of a powder.

The Elastic Roof Coating has been extensively used for many years, and has been found to be the most lasting and satisfactory ever manufactured, as, owing to its peculiar composition, it has never been known to crack or rub off, but retains its elastic and solid surface, perfectly impervious to water and thoroughly protecting the metallic surface from rust and leakage.

Architects and Builders are requested to give this paint a trial, as we feel very confident that its value will in every case be demonstrated by practical use.

Put up in Barrels and Half-Barrels, Kegs of 5 and 10 gallons, Cans of 1 gallon.

F. W. DEVOE & COMPANY,

(Established 1852.)

Offices: corner Fulton and William Streets, New York City,

MANUFACTURERS OF

THE HIGHEST GRADES OF

COACH, CAR AND CARRIAGE VARNISHES.

Our Varnishes have been long and favorably known by the Railway Car and Carriage Manufacturers throughout the United States, and are by them highly esteemed for their *ease of working, brilliancy and great durability.*

At different times some of the largest RAILWAY CORPORATIONS in the country have made elaborate and severe tests of the varnishes made by different manufacturers, and in every case the results of such tests have been in favor of the varnishes manufactured by F. W. DEVOE & COMPANY.

We claim that our varnishes are equal in quality to any manufactured in the United States or abroad. We do not spend large sums in extravagant methods of advertising, but market our goods on their merits alone.

DESCRIPTIVE LIST OF SOME OF OUR DIFFERENT MANUFACTURES:

WEARING BODY, or FINISHING, - $5.50
A very pale Varnish of great brilliancy and durability. Unsurpassed in its free working qualities. Dries dust free in 10 to 12 hours, and can be run out in 3 to 4 days.

MEDIUM DRYING BODY, - - - 5.00
Fully equal to our Finishing Body in paleness and freedom of working. Dries dust free in 10 hours, and can be run out in from 2 to 3 days.

HARD DRYING BODY, - - - 4.50
A pale and brilliant Varnish, working easily, and drying dust free in 6 to 8 hours. Can be used for hurried finishing.

WEARING CARRIAGE, or GEAR, - - 4.50
For finishing wheels and the under parts of carriages. A free working, rich lustre and durable Varnish.

ELASTIC CARRIAGE, - - - 4.00
A superior Varnish for finishing the under parts of carriages. Very light in color, good body; will dust-dry over night, and harden in 24 hours.

PALE RUBBING, or LEVELING, - - 4.25
Is quite pale, works freely and rubs easily. Will rub in 3 days without sweating.

QUICK RUBBING, - - - - $3.75
This Varnish is used for quick work, as its name indicates. Can be rubbed in from 36 to 48 hours, and will neither sweat nor crack.

BLACK RUBBING, - - - - 4.00
A Jet Black Rubbing Varnish. Works easily and can be rubbed in 48 hours.

ONE COAT COACH, - - - - 3.00
A heavy bodied, light colored Varnish. Works easily and gives a brilliant finish. Dries in 24 hours.

EXTRA No. 1 COACH, - - - 2.50
Heavy body; light color and quick drying; for general carriage undercoats and repairing. Dries hard in 12 hours.

No. 1 COACH, - - - - 2.00
Good body; light color; for carriage repair work, grained and inside work generally. Dries over night.

No. 2 COACH, - - - - 1.50
For general carriage work, painters' use, etc.

COACH PAINTERS' JAPAN, - - 1.75
For coach and car painters. A sure dryer and binder. Will mix readily with oil, and will not curdle.

BLACK ENAMEL LEATHER TOP, - 3.00
For refinishing old coach and carriage tops.

OUTSIDE CAR FINISHING, - - $5.50
This Varnish is intended for final or finishing coats on best passenger car work. Is very pale and durable; will resist the action of dust, cinders and rain. Dries dust free in 18 hours.

INSIDE CAR FINISHING, - - - 4.50
For finishing interior work of passenger cars. Very light color, heavy body, and dries thoroughly hard over night.

RAILWAY RUBBING, - - - 4.50
For undercoats on passenger cars. Can be rubbed in 2 days without sweating.

ENGINE FINISHING, - - - 5.00
A pale and free working Varnish. It is intended for finishing coats on engines. It dries over night, and can be run out in 3 days.

ENGINE RUBBING, - - - 4.50
For undercoats on engines. Can be rubbed in 24 hours.

BROWN DRYING JAPAN, - - - 1.50
A superior article for drying and binding colors.

BLACK JAPAN, - - - - - 1.50
A quick drying Black Japan, for use on smoke-stacks and all iron work on railway cars. Dries hard, with brilliant lustre.

F. W. DEVOE & COMPANY,

(ESTABLISHED 1852.)

Offices: corner Fulton and William Streets, New York City,

MANUFACTURERS OF

PASTE WOOD SURFACERS, OR FILLERS,

FOR LIGHT AND DARK WOODS.

These articles are superior to anything of the kind heretofore manufactured, from the fact that they thoroughly fill the pores of the wood and leave a *perfectly smooth finish*.

Many Fillers being largely composed of gritty substances, leave a rough, sandy surface, thereby preventing a perfect result after polishing or varnishing.

Our PASTE FILLERS, on account of their peculiar softness, are preferred by all who have given them a careful trial.

They are used by many of the leading Railway Companies and builders, who value them particularly on account of the superior results attained by their use.

We ask Architects and Builders to give the above their careful consideration.

DIRECTIONS :

Thin the Filler with Spirit Turpentine to the consistency of Heavy Body Varnish. If it sets too quick, add a little Raw Linseed Oil. Apply with ordinary paint brush (well worn), rubbing well into the wood. Allow it to set until it assumes a whitish appearance, which will be in from fifteen to twenty minutes; then scrape off with a square putty knife, or wipe off with rags or waste. The best result is gained by scraping.

Use a sharp stick to clean out the crevices in ornaments and mouldings. Allow the filled work to stand, after scraping and cleaning off, from eight to ten hours; then proceed to finish with Shellac or Varnish, as desired. Care must be taken not to go over more surface with the Filler than can be cleaned off before hardening.

F. W. DEVOE & COMPANY,

(Established 1852.)

Offices: corner Fulton and William Streets, New York City,

MANUFACTURERS OF

SUPERIOR WOOD COATING,

A brilliant and durable Finish and Protector for all kinds of hard and soft woods, either natural, painted or stained. It is highly recommended as a finish for churches, dwellings, public buildings, hospitals, floors, etc., used either on exterior or interior work.

No. 1 COATING, - - - $4.00.
DRIES IN 24 HOURS.

No. 2 COATING, - - - $2.75.
DRIES IN 12 HOURS.

These Coatings give a more BRILLIANT, HARD and ELASTIC surface than Hard Oil Finish, and although higher in price, will be found much more DURABLE and ECONOMICAL in the end; as, owing to the materials used in their manufacture, they will not *scratch* or *crack*, as is the case with many of the cheap articles.

We call the attention of ARCHITECTS and BUILDERS to the above, and ask them to give these their careful consideration.

DIRECTIONS:

On new work, fill the grain or pores of the wood with our "Paste Wood Surfacer" as per directions. When thoroughly dry, rub down with fine sand paper, and apply one coat of either No. 1 or No. 2 Coating, as circumstances permit; if a very high gloss is wanted, finish with No. 1 Coating. Care must be used to allow one coat to thoroughly harden before applying another. For last, or finishing coat on outside work, use No. 1 Coating.

F. W. DEVOE & COMPANY,

(Established 1852.)

Offices: corner Fulton and William Streets, New York City.

THE HIGHEST PREMIUM.

THE ONLY GOLD MEDAL

FOR

CAR BODY COLORS

GIVEN AT THE

National Exposition of Railway Appliances, held in Chicago, June, 1883,

WAS UNANIMOUSLY AWARDED TO F. W. DEVOE & COMPANY.

THE HIGHEST AWARD.

A SILVER MEDAL,

FOR OUR MANUFACTURE OF

PAINT, VARNISH AND ARTISTS'

BRUSHES.

At this Exposition our manufactures were subjected to the most severe tests, and the most searching criticisms, by specially appointed juries, composed of some of the most practical master car painters of the United States, and we are happy to state that we were unanimously awarded the above prizes, over all other competitors.

F. W. DEVOE & COMPANY.

COFFIN, DEVOE & COMPANY,

176 Randolph Street, Chicago, Ills.,

GENERAL WHOLESALE WESTERN AGENTS

FOR THE SALE OF

F. W. Devoe & Company's

MANUFACTURES.

————————— ——

Messrs. Coffin, Devoe & Company keep on hand a full and complete stock of our
PAINTS, VARNISHES, BRUSHES and ARTISTS' MATERIALS.

—————————

FREDERICK W. DEVOE,
President.

GORHAM B. COFFIN,
Vice-President.

J. SEYMOUR CURRY,
Secretary and Treasurer.

Color Analysis of the Fifty Paint Samples

COLOR	USE	PLATE
605	Body	XV
	Peaks, Shingle Work, Belts, and Sash	XV
661	Body	IX
659	(See alternate color schemes)	
654	Body	XI, XII
	Trim	V, VIII
585	Body	XVII
658	Body	II
660	(See alternate color schemes)	
533	(See alternate color schemes)	
651	Body	VIII, XII, XVI, XVIII, XX
	Trim	XVI, XVII, XIX
	Blinds	II, IV, V, VII, XV, XVII
	Sash	IX, XIV
	Peaks & Sides of Dormers	I
	Roof	II
656	Body	V
	Belt Course and Trim	XIV
582	Sash	II, XX
655	Sash	XV
664	(See alternate color schemes)	
662	Body	I
	Peaks & Sides of Dormers	II
525	Sash	XI, XII
609	Blinds	XVI
657	(See alternate color schemes)	
650	Body	XV
	Peaks & Gable Fronts	XV
604	(See alternate color schemes)	
653	Trim	X, XI
536	Trim	XVIII
663	Trim	IX
587	Body	XI
	Sash	III, XIX
	Roof	IX, XV
652	Trim	II, XII, XV, XX
	Blinds	I, IX, XIV, XV, XVI, XIX
	Sash	XVIII

COLOR	USE	PLATE
541	Body	III
584	(See Editor's Preface)	
607	(See alternate color schemes)	
530	(See alternate color schemes)	
601	(See alternate color schemes)	
580	Body	II, X
586	(See Editor's Preface)	
534	Trim	III, VI
	Sash	VI
610	(See alternate color schemes)	
611	Body	XIV
	Trim	XV
540	(See alternate color schemes)	
589	Body	XIV, XVI, XIX
	Trim	XVI
	Blinds	VIII, X, XVIII
	Sash	XVII
	Peaks & Gable Fronts, Shingle Work, and Belts	XVI
	Roof	XV, XVI
608	Body	I
	Trim	IV
	Sash	IV, V
591	Body	VI
595	Body	VII
	Sash	VII
581	Blinds	III
583	Sash	X
532	(See alternate color schemes)	
606	(See alternate color schemes)	
542	(See alternate color schemes)	
527	Trim	VII
588	Trim	I
	Blinds	XX
	Roof	VIII
526	Body	IV
539	Sash	VIII
597	(See alternate color schemes)	
544	Blinds	VI

Alternate Color Schemes Based on John Lucas & Co.,

Portfolio of Modern House Painting Designs, 1887

I. Body—658; Shutters & Trim—654; Shutter panels picked out—539; Roof shingles—542

II. Body—654; Shutters & Trim—539; Shutter panels—654; Sash & Door moldings—582; Roof shingles—542

III. Body—582; Shutters & Trim—532; Shutter panels—597; Sash & Shutter moldings—582; Roof shingles—597

IV. Body—597; Shutters & Trim—532; Sash & Shutter moldings—582; Roof shingles—582

V. Body—532; Trim—597; Shutter panels—532; Shutter moldings—582; Roof shingles—582

VI. Body—530; Trim—540; Sash & picking out—610; Roof shingles—534

VII. Body—610; Trim—527; Sash—610; Roof shingles—534

VIII. Body—660; Trim—659; Trim picked out—527; Sash—527; Roof shingles—582

IX. Body—611; Trim—609; Sash—611; Roof shingles—534 (slate)

X. Body—609; Trim—611; Sash—609; Roof shingles—534 (slate)

XI. Body—604; Trim—582; Trim picked out—653

XII. Body—653; Trim—604

XIII. Body—607; Trim—533; Roof shingles—527

XIV. Body—660; Trim—607; Shutters—660; Moldings of Shutters picked out—611; Sash—611; Roof shingles—609

XV. Body—526; Trim—664; Shutters & Moldings—607; Roof shingles—534 (slate)

XVI. Body—526; Trim—664; Moldings & Sash—606; Shutters—664; Panels—606*

XVII. Body—604; Trim—607; Shutters—604; Panels—607; Sash—607

XVIII. Body—657; Trim—610; Sash—654; Roof shingles—582

XIX. Body—604; Trim—580; Sash & Roof shingles—587; Foundation—605*

XX. Body—601; Trim—589; Sash—653; Roof shingles—587*

*Suggestions for combinations not given by Devoe or Lucas using colors from the Devoe line of paints.

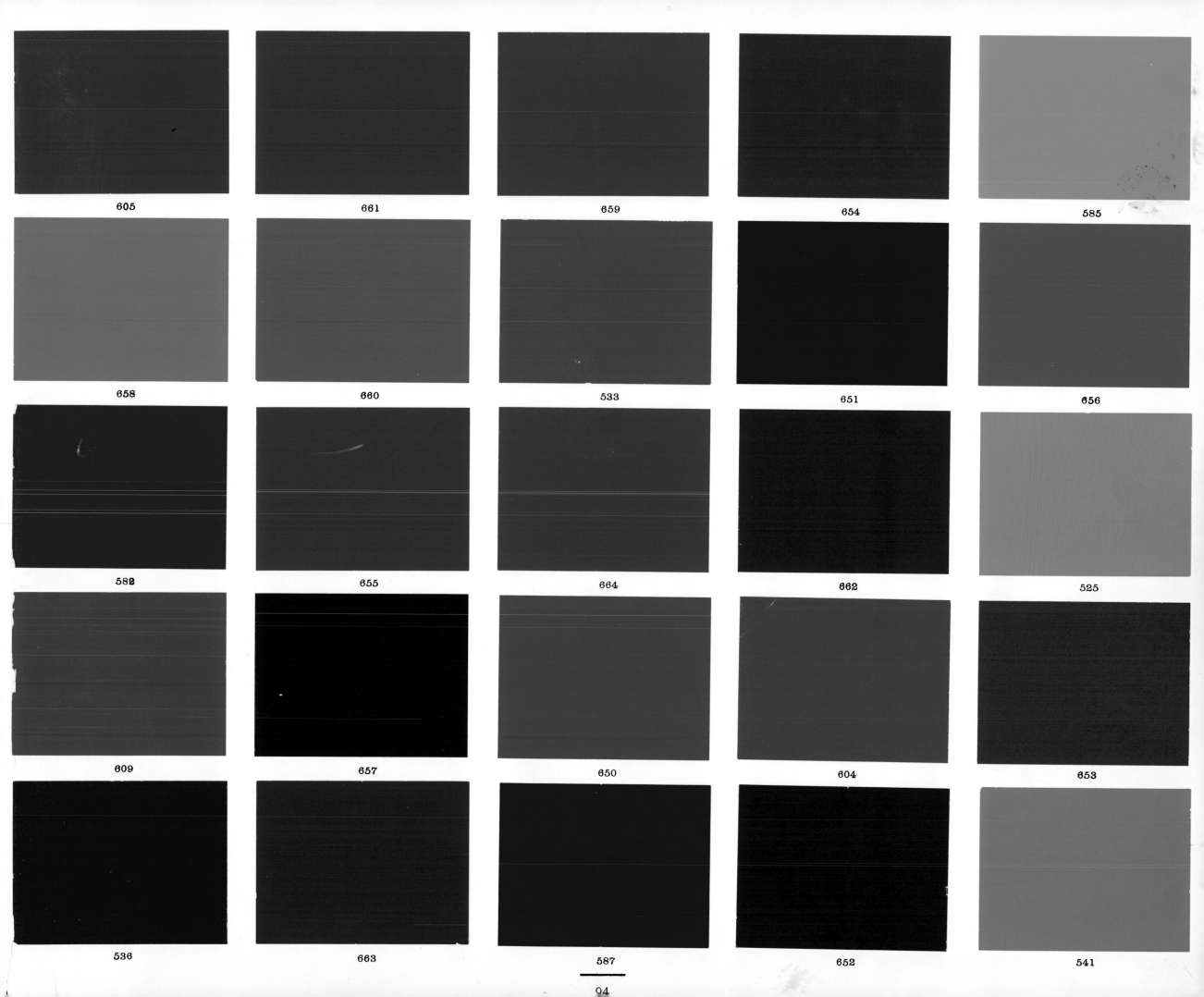

605

661

659

654

585

658

660

533

651

656

582

655

664

662

525

609

657

650

604

653

536

663

587

652

541

94

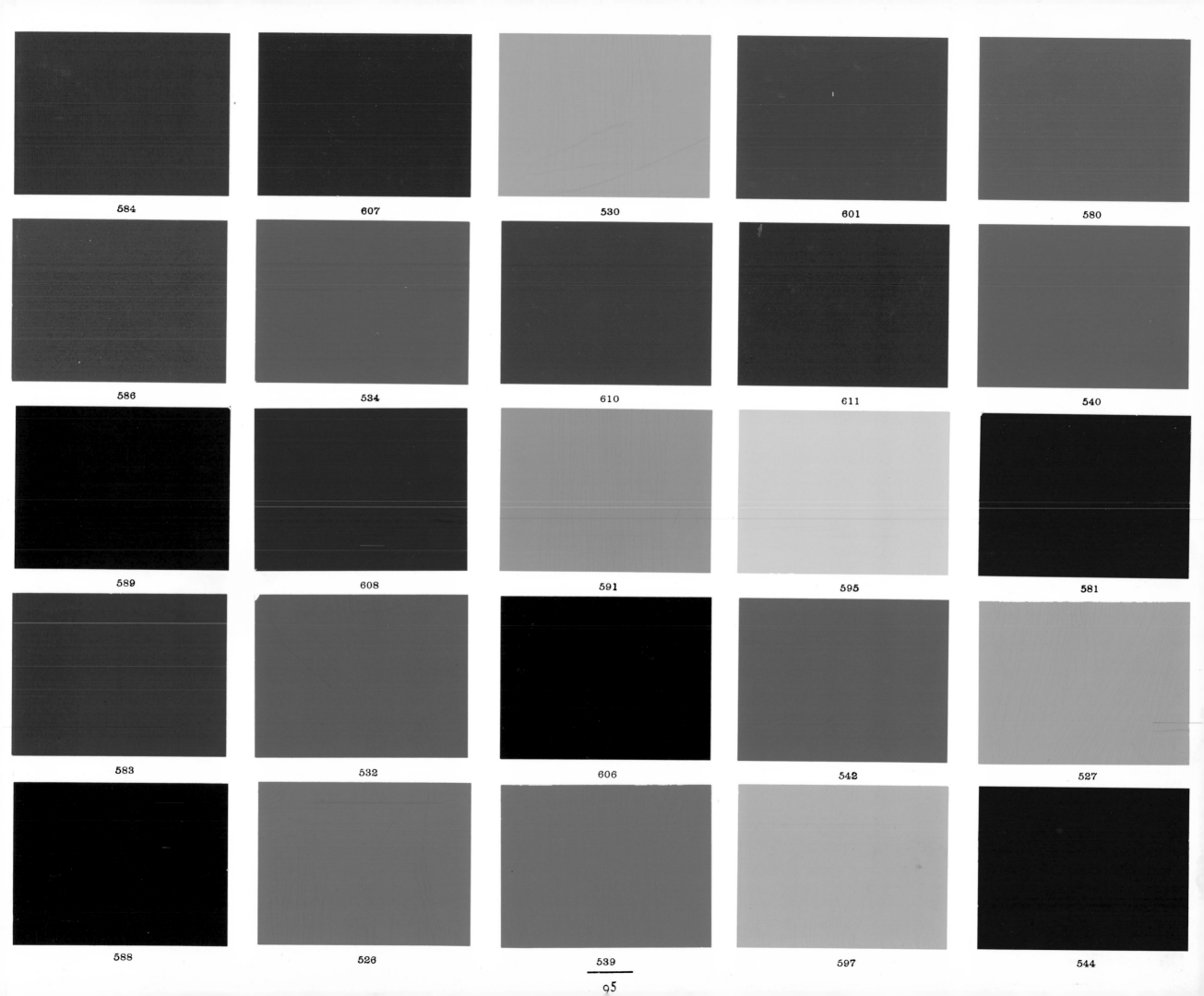

584

607

530

601

580

586

534

610

611

540

589

608

591

595

581

583

532

606

542

527

588

526

539

597

544